—— Making History ——
The Age of Empire

Making History

The Age of Empire

The British Overseas 1700 – 1900

John Patrick

Formerly Lecturer in History
Aberdeen College of Education

Mollie Packham

Formerly Head of History
Falmer School, Brighton

John Murray

Making History

Already published in this series

The Age of Invasions: Britain 55 BC–AD 1200
Struggles for Power: Britain 1300–1700
Years of Change: Britain 1700–the present

Cover: the British Empire in about 1900

Illustrations by Susan Bird

© Mollie Packham and John Patrick 1987

First published 1987
by John Murray (Publishers) Ltd
50 Albemarle Street, London W1X 4BD

Reprinted 1990

Typeset by Fakenham Photosetting Ltd
Printed and bound in Great Britain
at The Bath Press, Avon

British Library Cataloguing in Publication Data
Patrick, John, 1931–
    Age of empire: the British overseas
    1700–1900.—(Making history)
    1. Great Britain—Colonies—History
    —18th century 2. Great Britain—
    Colonies—History—19th century
    I. Title II. Packham, Mollie III. Series
    325'.32'0941   JV1011
    ISBN 0-71965-4307-X

Contents

Introduction

The *Making History* series does not set out to provide a continuous narrative covering the whole of British history. Instead it aims to study selected aspects of the history of Britain in the context of the wider world. It emphasises both the links which, throughout its history, have bound Britain to other countries, and the multicultural heritage of the British people.

Each of the first three books in the series has five main units linked by a broad common theme, an evidence-based inquiry, and investigative topic work. Each unit explores features of British life during a particular period, bringing it to life in a way that would be impossible in a general survey.

The Age of Empire, the third book in the series, highlights parts of the story of how the British built up their empire, how they made use of their new territories, and what happened to the people who lived in the countries under British rule. The first unit, *The British in North America*, shows how the British defeated the French in North America, why the colonists then rebelled, and how they won their independence. *The British West Indies* describes how the British used slaves to produce sugar for consumption in Britain, how slavery was abolished, and what happened to the West Indies afterwards.

The French Wars, 1793 – 1815 is an account of how Britain and her allies defeated the French in Europe, and how Britain used this success to add to her overseas empire, making up for the loss of the American colonies. *Conflicts in South Africa* tells the story of how two white powers, the Boers and the British, crushed the Zulu kingdom, and how the Boers eventually took control of South Africa. *The British in India* looks at British rule in India in the second half of the nineteenth century.

Each of these units follows the same basic pattern, opening with the vividly told story of an incident that sets the scene for the whole unit, leading to a structured sequence of carefully graded study work: *How do we know?*, *Understanding what happened*, and *Further work*. This is followed in each unit by further sequences of text and closely integrated study sections which are centred on the text, include evidence-based work, expand the themes and ideas contained in the text and also introduce new material—often reflecting contemporaneous events in Britain. The study sections will enable students to build on the skills that have been developed in the first two books of the series, and to continue to work towards an understanding of the terms and concepts they will meet when preparing for GCSE.

The Inquiry, *The Irish Potato Famine*, investigates the background to the Famine of 1846 and the British Government's attempts to deal with it. Pupils are provided with a wide range of evidence and are encouraged to evaluate it and come to their own conclusions. The *Topic work* that ends the book provides an opportunity to follow up some of the themes running through the book in more detail, and offers guidance on how to find and present material. Both this section and the Inquiry will further encourage the development of historical skills and the ability to carry out independent research.

The book attempts to encourage a balanced view of the process and consequences of empire-building, with the needs of today's multicultural society particularly in mind. Limitations of space have meant that it has not been possible to include a study of the last years of the Empire and the growth of the Commonwealth in this book, but it is hoped that a foundation has been laid on which teachers will be able to build to suit their own requirements. A study of the Commonwealth will be one of the themes of the fifth book in this series, *The Twentieth-Century World*.

It is hoped that pupils who use the first three volumes in the series, and who continue to study history, will acquire the skills they need to approach examination work with confidence, and that those who then cease to study the subject will have formed a coherent view of the making of the British people and gained some insight into the way history is written.

Notes for the teacher

The following notes may be helpful to teachers using this book.

Aims

The Age of Empire aims to develop the student's ability to use chronological conventions and put events in sequence, to make empathetic judgements, and to use historical concepts and skills (see *History in the Primary and Secondary Years: An HMI View* (1985)).

The skills used in studying history are interdependent and many of the study sections in this book require students to use a number of them together. However, throughout the book there are also studies that focus on a particular skill, for example:

1 Using Evidence

Study: *How do we know?* (pages 3, 26, 53, 82, 107)

These studies encourage the student to test the validity of the text of the preceding narrative, giving an account of, and extracts from, the sources on which it is based. A variety of written, statistical and visual evidence is used. The student is given practice in simple cross-referencing and extrapolation, and is introduced to such terms as 'bias' and 'primary and secondary sources'.

Another example of the use of evidence is found in the Study: *Photographs of India* (page 113). This shows how photographs can be edited to give a misleading impression.

2 Historical Empathy

Studies: *Use Your Imagination* (pages 10, 46, 73, 99, 119) (written work)
Should Richard Parker die? (page 63) (discussion)
Drama—the Great Trek (page 104)

These are designed to allow students 'to enter into some form of appreciation of the predicaments and points of view of other people in the past' (*History in the Primary and Secondary Years*, page 10). Other examples are to be found throughout the book.

3 Recording Information

Studies: Rival colonists in America (page 12)
Slave-trading (page 38)
Guarding the Channel (page 59)

These teach students to make brief notes on the concepts of cause and consequences. Techniques of note-making are developed throughout the book as a necessary preliminary to written work and discussion.

In Addition

1 The evidence-based *Inquiry* (pages 133–9) uses primary and secondary sources to lead students to investigate the causes of the Irish Potato Famine, the desperate situation of the Irish peasants, and the dilemma faced by the British Government.

2 The *Topic Work* section (page 140) gives advice on how to choose a subject for a study in depth, how to find information in books, and how to present the study in its final form. This will give students a thorough grounding in the kind of approach required for both GCSE course work and the examination itself.

Acknowledgements

The authors and publishers would like to thank Dr Martin Booth of Cambridge University Department of Education for his help in the preparation of this series.

Thanks are also due to Dr John Tosh of the Polytechnic of North London for his help and advice. The authors and publishers are grateful to the following for permission to reproduce copyright photographs:
p. 6, Peter Newark's Western Americana; pp. 8, 18(right), 19, 35, 43(both), 58, 60, 61, 65, 67, 72, 126, The Mansell Collection; p. 9, The Mary Evans Picture Library; pp. 13, 44, 45, The National Portrait Gallery; pp. 14, 16, 18(left), 22, 50, 51, 68, 69, 87, 97(top), The National Army Museum; pp. 30(both), 32, 80(bottom), 127, The Royal Commonwealth Society; pp. 37, 42, The Wilberforce Museum, Hull; pp. 52, 62, 92(top), The National Library of Scotland; p. 63, The Royal College of Surgeons of England; p. 71, City of Bristol Museum and Art Gallery; pp. 80(top), 88, The Africana Museum, Johannesburg; p. 81, The South African Library, Cape Town; p. 95, Studio Bassano; p. 97(bottom), BBC Hulton Picture Library; p. 101, Routledge & Kegan Paul Ltd; p. 102, Leicester University Press; pp. 106, 112, 113, 114, 116, 118, 121, 122, 128, The India Office Library; p. 110, Reproduced by gracious permission of Her Majesty The Queen; p. 130, Architectural Association.

The authors and publishers are also grateful to the following for permission to reproduce copyright material: p. 53, Elizabeth Longford, *The Years of the Sword*, George Weidenfeld & Nicolson Ltd; p. 135, Cecil Woodham Smith, *The Great Hunger*, Hamish Hamilton Ltd.

A note about money
Prices and wages have been left in pounds, shillings and pence (£.s.d.).
There were 12 pence in a shilling and 20 shillings in a pound.
The shilling has now become our 5p piece.

Wages and Prices 1700 – 1900 (in shillings and pence)

A carpenter's daily pay	Year	The price of a loaf of bread weighing 4 lb (2 kg)
1s 8d	1700	6½d
1s 10d	1750	4d
2s 0d	1800	1s 3½d
5s 0d	1850	8d
6s 0d	1900	5d

1 The British in North America

The Boston Tea Party

The town of Boston

In the eighteenth century Boston, the capital of Massachusetts, stood on a peninsula jutting out into a huge shallow bay dotted with islands. The bay formed a splendid harbour, and Boston was one of the busiest ports in America, with 600 cargo ships and a large fishing fleet. Trade made Boston rich. By 1760 it had nearly 20,000 inhabitants. They were proud of its paved streets, elegant squares and well-built houses. It had a good inn—the Green Dragon—and four newspapers. Boston people were tough and self-confident. They were also very religious. They held their Sunday services in 'meeting houses', which were among the largest buildings in the town.

The Thursday meeting

At ten o'clock in the morning on Thursday 16 December 1773, the Old South Meeting House was crammed to the doors with 5,000 excited citizens. They were not there to hold a service. Instead they were discussing tea, and they were very angry. The tea in question was lying in three ships, the *Dartmouth*, the *Eleanor* and the *Beaver*, alongside Griffin's Wharf in the outer harbour. Each ship held more than 100 chests of tea—in all about 45,000 kg, worth more than £9,000.

The tea had come from China. It had been shipped from Canton to London, and then from London to Boston, where it was now waiting to be unloaded. It was good tea. The people were angry because the British Parliament had put a tax on it. The tea merchants of Boston would have to pay a duty of 3 pence on every pound (450 g) before they could sell it to the public.

This duty annoyed the people of Boston. They believed that, as they had not elected any of the MPs, Parliament had no right to tax them. 'No taxation without representation' was their motto. For years they had tried to persuade the British Government not to tax them, and eventually the British had lifted all their taxes—except the duty on tea.

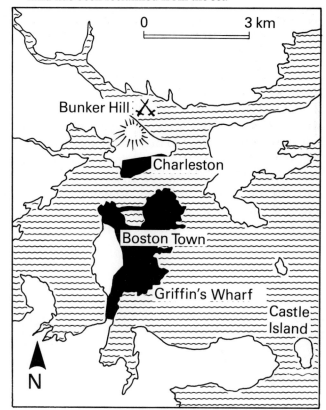

▼ Boston in the eighteenth century. Since then a lot of land has been reclaimed from the sea

'No' to the tea tax

The leaders of the citizens were determined not to pay the tea tax. So in the Meeting House, Sam Adams was busy persuading his angry fellow-citizens that the tea must be sent back to Britain. They agreed with him, and ordered Francis Rotch, the owner of the *Dartmouth*, to sail his ship with its cargo of tea back across the Atlantic.

Rotch refused. He said he did not dare leave harbour. He pointed out that according to the law, he ought to have paid the duty as soon as his ship entered port. If he tried to leave without paying, the British would certainly stop him. There were troops on Castle Island with cannon pointing out across the narrow passage out of the bay. They could easily stop his ship, or even sink it. Rotch said he would go if the Governor, Thomas Hutchinson, gave him permission. Otherwise his ship would stay put.

Adams and his friends did not try to persuade Rotch to change his mind. Instead they told him to go to Governor Hutchinson and ask for permission to sail. This was bound to take some time because the Governor was at his country house at Milton, 11 km away. So the meeting broke up for a few hours while Rotch set off in pouring rain on his long ride. At three o'clock the men returned to the Meeting House, but there was no sign of Rotch. Adams and the others passed the time in making speeches. They condemned tea-drinking, and declared that they would never allow the tea to come ashore.

Once again the hall was crowded. Most of those present were soberly dressed, but around the doors and in the gallery there were a few strange figures. They were obviously white men, but they had blackened their faces and wrapped blankets round their shoulders so that in the dark they could be mistaken for Indians. Inside the hall the speeches continued. Outside, the rain stopped, and it began to get dark. At a quarter to six there was a clatter of hoofs. Rotch was back.

Rotch refuses to sail

Rotch made his way into the hall. It was now quite dark, except for pools of light here and there where a few candles had been lit. He made his report. The Governor had refused to give him permission to sail, so his ship would stay where it was. Nobody was very surprised. They all knew that two of the Governor's sons were tea merchants who would make a good profit if the tea was landed and sold.

There was a great shout from the crowd in the hall, and when order had been restored Sam Adams rose and said, 'I do not see what else the inhabitants can do to save their country.' His words must have been a signal, for they were at once answered by a war-whoop from one of the 'Indians' in the gallery. This cry was repeated by those at the entrance. Others bellowed, 'Boston Harbour a teapot tonight!' and 'Hurrah for Griffin's Wharf!' as they dashed out into the street shouting and screaming. 'You would have thought the inhabitants of the infernal regions had broken loose,' said one onlooker.

▲ An American man and woman of about 1770

The tea goes overboard

With the men disguised as Indians in the lead, the crowd made its way through the streets down to Griffin's Wharf where the three ships lay at anchor. It was now a fine night, and the moon shone brightly as the 'Indians', who numbered about sixty, split into three groups. While the crowd watched quietly, they boarded the ships and forced the customs officers who were guarding the tea to go ashore. Then they set to work.

Some went below with lanterns and attached ropes to the tea-chests, one by one. Others hauled them up on deck. It was slow and difficult work, because each chest weighed about 200 kg. When the chests were on deck, the men broke them open with hatchets. Then they tipped the tea into the harbour, and threw the chests in after it.

The men worked steadily for about three hours. It was almost low tide, and at Griffin's Wharf the water was less than a metre deep. Gradually the tea began to pile up beside the ships, and the men had to push it aside to make room for more. They were very careful to make sure that none was stolen. At one point an Irishman named Connor, who made his living hiring out horses, was seen stuffing tea into the lining of his coat. The men seized him, tore his clothes off and rolled him in the mud.

By nine o'clock the gangs had finished. When they had tipped the last chest of tea into the harbour they clambered ashore. They had not touched any of the other cargo the ships were carrying. As the men came ashore the crowd broke up and went home.

So ended the famous Boston Tea Party. Nobody now knows the names of the men who took the tea and tipped it into the harbour. But we do know quite a lot about what happened that day, thanks to a letter written at the time.

Study 1

How do we know?

John Andrews's letter

John Andrews was a citizen of Boston, and was there on 16 December 1773 when the Boston Tea Party took place. Andrews knew that his brother, who did not live in Boston, would hear all kinds of rumours, so on 18 December he wrote him a long letter, describing what had really happened. Some parts of the story of the Boston Tea Party are based on this letter.

1 Why would you expect John Andrews
  to know what happened in Boston on 16 December 1773,
  to remember the events clearly when he wrote to his brother?

2 In his letter, John Andrews says that he was at home on the afternoon of 16 December when he heard an uproar coming from the Old South Meeting House. What are we told in the story to suggest that this uproar broke out when Rotch reported that the Governor would not give him permission to sail?

3 John Andrews says that he could not believe it when he heard that the demonstrators were marching to Griffin's Wharf, so he went to see for himself. He states that the demonstrators
  took great care not to damage any cargo apart from the tea,
  did not harm the ships' crews or officers.
Do these statements suggest that the demonstrators were
  a violent, uncontrolled mob,
  a disciplined group who used a limited amount of force to make their point?
Give reasons for your answer.

What do you think?

Who would find John Andrews's letter more useful:
  a historian studying the causes of the Boston Tea Party,
  a historian trying to decide how much violence took place at Griffin's Wharf?
Give reasons for your answer.

→

3

Part of a leaflet given out in Boston

Boston, December 2 1773

. . . This is to Remind the Public that it was solemnly voted by the Body of the People of this and neighbouring towns assembled at the Old South Meeting House on Tuesday the 30th Day of November that . . . tea never should be landed in the Province or pay a Farthing of Duty.

The People

Printed on the presses supporting the Sons of Liberty.

What are we told in the leaflet which helps to confirm that

the Old South Meeting House was used for public meetings,

many people in and around Boston objected to the tax on tea,

Sam Adams's words, 'I do not see what else the inhabitants can do to save their country', were probably a signal that had been arranged before the meeting?

Understanding what happened

1 Copy the table below and fill in the missing times and words with the help of the information that you are given in the story of the Boston Tea Party.
2 Write out these sentences, using the words below to fill in the gaps correctly:

representative governor capital Army
colony

Boston was the _____ of Massachusetts, a British _____ in America. The _____ was the King of Great Britain's _____ in the colony, and soldiers of the British _____ guarded the entrance to Boston Harbour.

3 The British Government claimed the right to tax all goods entering the American colonies. They had agreed to remove all the taxes except the one on tea.
   (a) Why did the Government remove most of the taxes?
   (b) What was the point of charging a tax on tea?
   (c) Why did the Bostonians refuse to pay any tax at all on tea?

Events of the Boston Tea Party, 16 December 1773

Time	Event
10 a.m.	5,000 citizens meet at the Old _____ Meeting House to stop the cargoes of _____ being unloaded. Sam _____ sends Captain _____ to ask the _____ to give him permission to sail back to England. The meeting breaks up.
_____	The protesters _____ again. Some come disguised as Indians.
_____	Rotch returns _____ permission to sail. The crowd goes to _____ Wharf.
6 p.m. – 9 p.m.	'Indians' tip tea into _____ Harbour.

Further work

Writing

1 Write a one-page leaflet that might have been given out by the Sons of Liberty, urging the Bostonians to attend the meeting to be held in the Old South Meeting House on 16 December 1773. Say why the meeting is being held, and give the names of the speakers.

2 Write the letter that one of the following men might have written to his family, describing how he spent Thursday, 16 December 1773:

> Sam Adams   Captain Rotch
> an 'Indian'

Mention:
> the meeting at the Old South Meeting House,
> the disturbances at Griffin's Wharf.

3 Write the report that the Governor of Massachusetts might have sent to King George III, describing
> the unrest in Boston in December 1773,
> his interview with Rotch on 16 December 1773,
> the events at Griffin's Wharf.

Drawing

1 (a) Draw the map of Boston on page 1.
  (b) Explain why each of these places was important in the story of the Boston Tea Party:
> The Old South Meeting House
> Griffin's Wharf
> Castle Island.

2 Draw a picture to illustrate this newspaper headline: 'Boston Harbour a teapot tonight!'

3 In 1773 the Boston newspapers often published cartoons showing Americans refusing to drink tea while it was taxed. The people in the cartoons were drawn with balloons coming out of their mouths, containing the words they were supposed to be saying.
  (a) Look at the picture of the American man and woman on page 2.
  (b) Draw a cartoon that might have been published in 1773 under the heading 'Teatime in Boston'.

Drama

In groups of three:

1 Each choose one of these people, and write the speech he might have made at the Old South Meeting House on 16 December 1773:
> Sam Adams—stating why he opposed the tea tax and urging everyone to stop the cargoes of tea from being landed,
> A citizen of Boston—saying why he thought the British Government had too much power over the American colonists,
> Captain Rotch—reporting that the Governor would not give him permission to take his cargo back to Britain and saying why he would have to unload it.

2 Rehearse your scenes in your groups.

3 Choose one group to make their speeches to the class, who form the audience at the Old South Meeting House.

4 After Captain Rotch has spoken, Sam Adams can say, 'I do not see what else the inhabitants can do to save their country,' and the audience can reply with war cries before the meeting is closed.

Making a history glossary

A history glossary is a collection of words that you need to use and understand when you study history.

1 Take a double page, either in the middle, or at the end, of your exercise book, and divide it up like this:

2 Begin your glossary by writing *tax* in the first 'Word' column.

3 In the first 'Meaning' column, use your own words to explain what a tax is.

4 Add these words to your glossary:
> representative   slogan

History glossary			
Word	Meaning	Word	Meaning

The American colonies

▼ The Thirteen Colonies

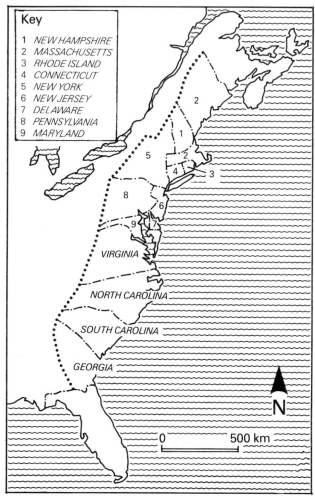

Key
1 NEW HAMPSHIRE
2 MASSACHUSETTS
3 RHODE ISLAND
4 CONNECTICUT
5 NEW YORK
6 NEW JERSEY
7 DELAWARE
8 PENNSYLVANIA
9 MARYLAND

Some Indians lived in caves; others lived in cabins or tents made of hide. Some tribes were ruled by chiefs, while others were governed by councils. Some thought the sun was God. Others worshipped the bison they hunted, or the maize that they grew. Some never went to war. Others spent most of their time fighting.

Each tribe had its own land, where the men hunted for bison, deer, bears, wild turkeys, partridges and pigeons. The tribes also had their own rivers, where the Indians caught fish by spearing or netting them.

The Indians hunted with bows, arrows and stone-headed axes called *tomahawks*: they had no guns. They kept a careful watch on their hunting-grounds, to make sure that no other tribe tried to take them over, for they depended on the animals they killed for their food and clothing.

The Thirteen Colonies

In the middle of the eighteenth century Britain had thirteen colonies in America. They stretched down the east coast from Massachusetts and New Hampshire in the north to Georgia in the south, a distance of more than 2,000 km. Virginia, the oldest colony, had first been settled in 1584. Georgia, the most recent, had been founded in 1733.

The American Indians

When the English reached North America, they found that there were already people living there —the American Indians. There had been Indians in America for at least 150,000 years. They lived in tribes, each with its own language, beliefs and way of life.

▲ Red Cloud was Chief of the Sioux in 1870. He once said, 'The white man made us many promises, more than I can remember, but they never kept but one; they promised to take our land, and they took it.'

When the first settlers arrived, the Indians were not alarmed. There were very few white men, and there seemed to be enough land for everyone. And the white men brought useful things such as guns and iron tools, which they were willing to trade for food or furs. So at first the colonists and the Indians usually lived at peace with each other.

The colonists take over

Gradually the number of colonists increased. They fenced off parts of the Indians' hunting-grounds to grow crops, and they killed animals which the Indians believed belonged to them. As a result, some Indians decided to get rid of the newcomers and began to attack their settlements.

In 1620 the Alconquians made a surprise attack on the English settlers in Virginia, and killed 347 of them before they were driven back.

The Indians had very few guns, and as a rule they were no match for the well-armed English settlers. So the settlements grew. The colonists continued to take Indian land for their crops, driving the tribes further inland.

Most colonists did not see anything wrong in taking land from the tribes. It did not occur to them that the Indians had a right to their own way of life. Instead the colonists thought of them as ignorant savages, and killed them without mercy. They did not realise that each tribe had its own history and traditions.

Study 2

Indian pictograms

Most of what we know about the Indians comes from accounts that the settlers wrote about them, but now this is changing. Indians are beginning to write their history from their own point of view. To do this, they are collecting together the stories that were passed down to them by their ancestors, and writings which we think date from the eighteenth century. These writings were so important to the Indian tribes that they wrapped them in the bundles in which they kept their most sacred possessions.

The Indians did not have an alphabet. Instead, they wrote in *pictograms* or word-pictures. For example, when an Indian scribe wanted to write 'warrior', he drew a man, rather like a pin man, holding a bow and arrow. To write 'chief', he drew a man wearing a feathered war bonnet, and holding the long-stemmed pipe that Indians smoked at important meetings.

Time was measured by the waxing and waning of the moon, that is, in months. When a scribe wanted to write the date he drew a half-moon and added a pictogram to show which month he was writing about. July was Heat Month, so its pictogram was the sun, which the scribe drew as a circle with wavy lines coming from it. September was Hunting Month, so its pictogram was a bow and arrow.

1 (a) What two kinds of information are Indians today collecting in order to write their own history?
  (b) Draw the pictogram for Heat Month.
  (c) Why did Indians draw a moon when they wrote the date?
2 (a) Draw the pictogram for Hunting Month.
  (b) Give three examples of animals that the Indians hunted.
  (c) Why did the Indians lose part of their hunting-grounds when the number of colonists increased?
3 (a) Copy the heading and list of dates below.

  English settlements in North America
  1584
  1620
  1733

  (b) Write brief notes against each date, saying why it was important in the history of English settlement in North America.
  (c) Draw some pictograms showing *either* a group of Indians trading with the settlers *or* an Indian raid on an English settlement.

Life in the colonies

The southern planters

In the south, the colonists made a living by growing tobacco on large plantations along the river-banks. When the tobacco had been cut and dried they sold it to English and Scottish merchants, who sailed up the rivers to collect it, and took it back to sell in Britain.

In the first half of the seventeenth century, more men than women went to settle in the southern colonies. So the company that bought and sold the tobacco shipped young women out from Britain to marry the planters. Company officials tried to make sure that the women were not forced to marry men they did not like. The officials also had to collect 55 kg of tobacco from each new husband, to pay the cost of his wife's voyage from Britain.

The planters needed people to work on their plantations. At first they paid the fare for labourers to come out from Britain. The labourers had to promise to work on the plantations for at least four years, and to pay back their passage-money. They had a hard life, but some managed to pay back what they owed and save a little money. Land was cheap, so they could buy plots for themselves and set up as planters. For instance, Adam Thoroughgood arrived in Virginia as a labourer in the second half of the seventeenth century. Fifteen years later he owned a plantation of 2,000 ha.

There were never enough labourers from Britain to work on the plantations, so the planters bought black slaves who had been shipped across from Africa. The number of black slaves increased steadily. By 1750 they made up half the population.

The slaves did all the work, so the planters had an easy life. A traveller in South Carolina said that they spent their time 'eating, drinking, lolling and smoking', while their wives were fond of dancing 'Negro jigs'. They were very extravagant, and most of them owed money to the merchants who bought their tobacco. A clergyman who visited Virginia in the middle of the eighteenth century said the people were 'uncultured', and found the only college in the state 'disappointing'.

The northern farmers

The northern colonies were quite different. The climate was too cold to grow tobacco, so the

▲ Slaves' living-quarters on a southern plantation. (An early photograph)

colonists cultivated maize, wheat, rye and barley. They hunted in the woods for turkey and wild pig, and they fished off the coast for cod. They sold dried fish and salt pork to the southern planters to feed their slaves. They built their own ships from the timber in the forests, and grew hemp to make rope for their boats. By the end of the seventeenth century, they had built up a steady trade carrying African slaves and West Indian rum. So they had become traders as well as farmers.

The colonists in the north had to work very hard. At harvest-time whole families had to work in the fields. But for most of the year the men cultivated the crops and hunted, while the women looked after the children and prepared all the meals. They also tended the cattle and hens which provided them with milk and eggs.

Most of the first settlers were Puritans, who went to America because they disagreed with the way the Church of England was organised. In America they established a system which suited them. In each community a few men set up a church and elected a minister. Then these 'brethren', as they were called, interviewed all the other members of the community, asking them about their beliefs and their private lives, to see if they were true believers. If the brethren were satisfied, they allowed them to join the church.

The power of the church brethren

The brethren had great power. They alone could vote, and they made the laws. They sent men to prison for singing rude songs, and put boys in the stocks for laughing and joking near the church. They refused to allow people with other beliefs to worship freely. This angered many newcomers. One said, 'I came from England because I did not like the Lord Bishops, but I cannot join with you because I would not be under the Lord Brethren.'

The northern colonists encouraged education. Every village had a school to teach reading and writing. Every town had a school where Latin grammar was taught. At Harvard a college was set up to train preachers. So the New Englanders, as they called themselves, were well educated.

The middle colonies

Between the southern colonies and New England there were five 'middle colonies'—Pennsylvania, New York, New Jersey, Delaware and Maryland. In the middle colonies, life was more easy-going than in New England. People were allowed to worship as they pleased, and there were all kinds of churches and chapels. The colonists made a good living from farming and trade. They built handsome, prosperous towns with good schools and pleasant taverns where the citizens could meet to play cards or discuss the latest news.

▲ The Allyn House in Massachusetts, built in about 1680.
Many New England farmhouses looked like this

Use your imagination

1 Caleb Rogers, a British colonist in America, has just got married. He could not find a job in Britain so he sailed to Virginia to work on a tobacco plantation. Tell his story from the day he arrived on the plantation to his wedding day ten years later.

Mention:
> the kind of life the plantation owner led,
> why Caleb could not leave the plantation for four years,
> how Caleb bought land and slaves and set up his own plantation, and paid for a woman to come from Britain to marry him.

(Think of something that you did that was hard at first but which made life better for you in the long run.)

2 Rachel Watson is a young widow with one son. It was hard for her to find a job in England because she is a Puritan, so she left her village and went to America to work on a farm in a northern colony. Tell her story from the day she arrived on the farm to the day her son, who wanted to be a Puritan preacher, left to go to Harvard.

Mention:
> the farm and her work there,
> the church she attended and how it was governed,
> her son's education and why he was put in the stocks.

(Think of something hard you decided to do for the sake of someone you loved.)

3 Samuel Bridger is the younger son of a wealthy Bristol merchant. He wanted to settle in America, and his father agreed to buy him some land there. Samuel spent some time travelling through the colonies before he decided where he wanted to live. Tell his story from the day he arrived in Boston to the day he bought his land.

Mention:
> his visit to a northern farm and a southern plantation,
> what he liked and disliked about life in the north and south,
> his reason for deciding to settle where he did.

(Think of a time when you could choose what you wanted and tried to make sure that you made the right choice.)

European colonies in America

The colonists and Britain

The Thirteen Colonies were quite separate from one another. Each had its own assembly elected by the citizens, its own law, its own money and its own customs. Though most colonists agreed that they were subjects of the British king, they did not think that the British Parliament had any rights over them. This was why they hated paying taxes to Britain.

The colonists also quarrelled with Britain about trade. They had plenty of timber and tobacco to sell, and in return they needed to buy manufactured goods such as iron pots and good quality cloth. The British Government knew that merchants could make money buying and selling in the colonies, and wanted to make sure that all the profits came back to Britain. So Parliament passed the Navigation Acts, which made it illegal for any foreign country to trade with the colonies. The colonists hated this. They wanted to trade with other European countries and with the nearby French and Spanish colonies.

Some colonists were so annoyed that they ignored the Navigation Acts, and smuggled goods to other countries. The British tried to stop them, but did not have enough ships and men to check every boat that sailed to and from America. So smuggling continued, much to the annoyance of the British.

But though the colonists grumbled, they did not quarrel openly with Britain, because they relied on British troops to defend them if they were attacked.

Spanish and French colonies

Spain and France also had colonies in North America. The Spanish had moved north from Mexico, and had landed in Florida and occupied it. The French had sailed up the St Lawrence River in Canada, settled on its banks, and defeated the Iroquois Indians who lived there. Then they had moved south, down the Mississippi Valley to the Gulf of Mexico, building a chain of forts which prevented the English colonists from exploring the west.

Most French colonists who came down the Mississippi were hunters and trappers. They

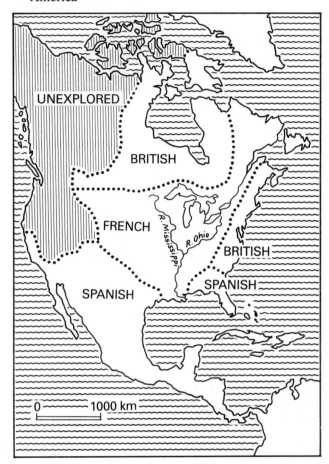

▼ British, French and Spanish colonies in North America

made their living by selling furs. They did not settle in one place, but travelled through the woods until they found a place where bears or beavers were plentiful. Then they pitched camp and set their traps. They knew that the Indians were skilled hunters, and respected them. If a trapper met a band of Indians he gave them presents of knives or axe-heads, and asked them where he should set his traps. So the French were on good terms with the Indians. Some French trappers married Indian women.

As the French moved south and established their forts, the British colonists became very uneasy. They feared that the French and Indians might join forces and attack the British colonies. So they appealed to Britain for help, and the Government sent troops across the Atlantic to defend the colonies.

Study 4

Rival colonists in America

The symbol ∴ is the abbreviation for *because*. You will save time if you *abbreviate*, that is, write as briefly as possible, when you are making notes.

1 (a) Read the section headed 'The colonists and Britain' on page 11.
  (b) Copy the notes below and complete them, using the abbreviation for *because*. For example, the first note to be completed begins:

> The colonists hated paying taxes to Br...

  You might complete this by adding:

> ∴ they did not think the Br Parlt had the right to tax them.

  <u>Quarrels between the British Government and the colonists</u>

> The colonists hated paying taxes to Br...
>
> The Br passed the Navigation Acts, making it illegal to trade with foreign countries...
>
> The colonists hated the Navigation Acts...
>
> They did not quarrel openly with Br...

2 (a) Read the section headed 'Spanish and French colonies' on page 11.
  (b) Copy and complete the notes below, using the abbreviation for *because*.

  <u>The French in America</u>

> The Br could not explore the west of America...
>
> Most Fr col did not settle in one place...
>
> The Fr respected the Ind...
>
> The Br became uneasy when the Fr moved S and built forts...

3 The notes below are about some people called the Metis.
  (a) Read the notes carefully and turn them into a paragraph by writing the information given in sentences.

  <u>The Metis</u>

> Live along Canadian – US border.
>
> Many have Fr surnames ∴ descended fr Fr fur-traders who married Ind wives.
>
> Met think of themselves as Ind but many customs and cooking are Fr.

  (b) Look at the map of English, French and Spanish colonies in America on page 11. Using the abbreviation ∴ , write notes explaining why a number of towns along the St Lawrence and Mississippi rivers have French names.

The Seven Years War

War breaks out

War first broke out between French and British colonists in 1747, when the French captured and destroyed a fort built by the British in the Ohio Valley. On its site the French built a new fort, called Fort Duquesne after one of their admirals.

In 1755 war broke out again when British colonists tried to drive the French out of Fort Duquesne. They sent a small force under the command of Colonel George Washington, but it was defeated. So in July General Braddock set out with 1,500 British and colonial troops to capture the fort. They were marching along, 10 km from Duquesne, when suddenly they were fired on by Frenchmen and Indians who were hiding in the woods at the side of the road. Braddock was helpless. He could not see who was firing, and when his men charged into the woods to look for the enemy, they were shot as they stumbled through the undergrowth.

By the end of the day Braddock was fatally injured, and more than three-quarters of his troops had been killed or wounded. 'Who would have thought it?' whispered one dying officer.

Pitt's war policy

In 1757 a new Government was formed in Britain with William Pitt as chief minister. He took charge of the War. He worked out that the British forces in North America were much larger than the French, and he decided to capture all the French possessions there. So he ordered the British troops to attack.

In 1758 General Forbes led a British army over mountains and through thick forests to attack and capture Fort Duquesne. He renamed it Fort Pitt, and the city of Pittsburgh now stands on the site. A year later, in 1759, General Amherst captured Fort Ticonderoga, and began to advance towards the French settlement at Montreal.

The capture of Quebec

General Wolfe

Pitt's most important aim was to capture Quebec, the largest town in French Canada. He chose General James Wolfe to lead the attack. Wolfe was just over thirty. He was tall, thin and often ill. He worked hard, and was very intelligent. He thought his fellow officers were 'blunderers' who spent too much time drinking and gambling. When one of them had his head shattered by a cannonball, Wolfe looked at him and said, 'I never knew before that the fellow had so many brains.' Most army officers disliked Wolfe, and one told George II that the young man was mad. The King answered, 'Mad, is he? Then I hope he will bite some of my other generals.'

The defences of Quebec

Quebec was a well-built town overlooking the St Lawrence River. It was defended by 16,000 French troops, who were commanded by General Montcalm. At the end of June 1759 the British Navy landed Wolfe with 9,000 men on the opposite bank of the river. For two months Wolfe tried to find a way to capture Quebec.

His patrols found that the town itself was too strong to attack, and as his men explored the woods around Quebec, some of them were pounced on by Indians, killed and scalped. Wolfe's men were trained to fight battles on open ground, where they could see their enemies and advance together in line. They could not deal with sudden surprise attacks by men hidden in the undergrowth.

The Heights of Abraham

Just behind Quebec, on the top of a plateau called the Heights of Abraham, there was an open plain. Wolfe knew that if he could get his men formed up on this plain, facing the rear of Quebec where the town's defences were weak, Montcalm would have to lead the French Army out to try to drive the British away. This was the kind of battle that the British could win.

So Wolfe looked for a safe way up the north bank of the St Lawrence onto the Heights of Abraham. All the obvious paths were well guarded, but in September his scouts found a narrow path, hidden by trees, that wound up the bank to the top, about a kilometre from Quebec. Montcalm thought the British were very unlikely to use this path, so there were only a couple of sentries guarding it.

▲ General Wolfe was born in Kent in 1727. He joined the Army when he was fourteen, and fought in his first battle at sixteen. He was made a general at the age of 32

British naval officers had carefully charted the river, and they assured Wolfe that they could ship troops across and land them at the bottom of the path. Nevertheless, it was very dangerous to send an army over the St Lawrence in small boats and up a narrow path. If the French found out what was happening, they would be able to ambush the British and wipe them out as they were climbing out of the boats or struggling up the path.

Wolfe captures Quebec

Wolfe understood the danger, but decided that he had to take the risk. If he did not capture Quebec before the autumn, he would either have to retreat, or spend the winter in enemy country, cut off from the Navy by the ice that would gradually block the St Lawrence.

So on 13 September Wolfe launched his attack. At one o'clock in the morning, boats full of troops drifted quietly down the river on the tide. A French sentry on the bank spotted one of them and challenged it. A British officer who spoke French answered that it was a supply boat on its way to Quebec. The sentry believed him.

The boats ran aground at the foot of the path, and the men stepped ashore. A few of them crept up the path, attacked the sentries and killed them. Then a steady stream of men trudged up the dark path to the Heights 50 m above the river. Further downstream, British ships bombarded Quebec to distract the French. When dawn broke 4,500 British troops were lined up ready for battle.

As soon as Montcalm realised what had happened he led his army out onto the plains and attacked. The British held their fire until the enemy were only 50 m away. Then they fired. Many Frenchmen, including Montcalm, were killed. Hundreds were wounded and the rest fled. The British had won. But Wolfe was lying on the battlefield with a bullet in his chest. As the French retreated he died, murmuring, 'Now God be praised I will die in peace.' A few hours later his troops occupied Quebec.

The Peace of Paris

In September 1760 Amherst captured Montreal, leaving France's two main bases in Canada in British hands. But the Seven Years War between Britain and France—which was being fought in Europe and India as well as America—went on until 1763, when the Treaty of Paris granted Britain the whole of Canada. The power of the French in North America had been broken.

▲ This is a famous eighteenth-century engraving of the capture of Quebec, but the scale is wrong. The boats are far too large, and the banks are not high enough

Study 5

Celebrating a British victory

Whenever the news of a British victory reached London, the actors at the theatres celebrated it by putting on a *tableau vivant* or living picture of the battle scene.

If the victory had been won on land, a backcloth with a battlefield painted on it was lowered onto the stage. Actors dressed as soldiers, in red tunics, white knee-breeches and long black boots, leaned wearily on their muskets or knelt beside their wounded comrades. When a victory at sea was announced, 'sailors', in loose-fitting shirts and trousers, would stage a mock battle in front of painted waves and cut-out prows of ships. The roar of cannon-fire sounded from offstage.

In 1759 the British captured most of the important towns in Canada from the French. They also defeated a French fleet. To celebrate this wonderful year of victories, David Garrick, the actor-manager of the Theatre Royal, Drury Lane, wrote this song, with a chorus that all the audience could join in:

> Come cheer up my lads, 'tis to glory we steer
> To add something more to this wonderful year.
> 'Tis to honour we call you, as free men, not slaves,
> For who are so free as the sons of the waves?
> *Chorus*
> Hearts of oak are our ships, jolly tars are our men.
> We always are ready.
> Steady, boys, steady.
> We'll fight and we'll conquer again and again.

---

1 (a) Copy and illustrate the chorus of *Hearts of Oak*.
  (b) Why was 1759 a 'wonderful year' for the British?
2 (a) Draw a tableau showing General Wolfe dying at Quebec in his moment of victory.
  (b) Why was it important to the British to capture Quebec?

3 A tableau might include actors and actresses dressed to represent Britannia or Victory, or to look like the people of the country where the battle was fought.
  (a) Draw a tableau put on to celebrate 'Victory in Canada'.
  (b) Why, after the Peace of Paris in 1763, were French settlers in Canada ruled by Britain?

The War of American Independence

The colonists quarrel with Britain
The British colonists were glad that the French had been defeated. They thought that they would now be able to move west into the country which the French trappers had colonised. To their annoyance, the British Government ordered them to stay where they were. Britain had already spent well over £1 million on the War in America, and the Government did not want to spend even more money fighting Indians so that the colonists could take over more land for themselves.

In fact the British had decided it was time for the colonists to pay part of the cost of keeping British troops in America. The colonists refused. They no longer needed the British Army to defend them against the French, and they knew that British troops were not trained to fight against Indian raids and ambushes. So they had nothing to lose by defying the Government.

The majority of British MPs were shocked by the colonists' attitude, and they decided to tax the colonies. This annoyed the colonists, particularly the New England merchants who were already irritated by the effects of the Navigation Acts on trade.

These merchants were in America because in the past, a king of England had refused to allow their ancestors to reform the Church of England. The eighteenth-century colonists had no respect for kings, and had no intention of paying taxes to George III, particularly when the taxes had been voted by a Parliament thousands of miles away, in which the colonists were not represented. Neither side would give way. The British imposed taxes. The colonists refused to pay them. Then in 1773 came the Boston Tea Party (see page 1).

▲ An American engraving showing 'The Boston Massacre'. In March 1770, a crowd began to jeer and throw snowballs at a sentry guarding the customs house in Boston. Soldiers were sent to help him. They fired on the crowd, and killed five men

Study 6

Unrest in America

1 Complete the sentence below by copying the *two* statements that are correct:

    After the French in America were defeated, the British Government
- spent over £1 million on training an army to fight the Indians,
- would not allow the colonists to move west,
- thought the colonists should pay taxes towards the cost of keeping a British army in America.

2 Complete the sentence by copying the *four* statements that are correct:

    The American colonists
- wanted to move westward, even if it meant fighting the Indians,
- formed their own army to fight against the French,
- thought they no longer needed the British Army to protect them,
- disliked the Navigation Acts which prevented them from trading freely with foreign countries,
- objected to paying taxes to the British Parliament because they were not represented in it.

3 (a) In 1773 the slogan of the Sons of Liberty in Boston was 'No taxation without representation'.
   (i) What tax did they refuse to pay?
   (ii) Why, in 1773, would it have been difficult to send representatives of the American colonists to the Parliament in Britain?

  (b) At the Old South Meeting House, just before the 'Indians' set out for Griffin's Wharf, Sam Adams said, 'I do not see what else the inhabitants can do to save their country.'
    What do you think that Sam Adams and the Sons of Liberty believed they were saving their country from?

The coming of war

The punishment of Boston

The Boston Tea Party angered the British Government, and they decided to punish the people of Massachusetts. The Government knew that the prosperity of Boston depended on fishing and trade. They decided to close Boston Harbour to all shipping until the town paid the total cost of the tea that had been lost—including the tax. They also took away much of the power of the Massachusetts Assembly, and appointed a soldier, General Gage, as governor, with orders to station troops in the town of Boston.

Most British MPs agreed with the Government, but some did not. In the House of Lords, Pitt said that the idea of punishing the colonists was 'ruinous'. In the House of Commons, Edmund Burke told ministers it would not work because 'the fierce spirit of liberty' was stronger in America than anywhere else. In Boston, General Gage agreed. 'It is a great folly,' he wrote as his troops pitched their tents in the town. 'I fear the people will resist to the death.'

Gage was right. The Massachusetts colonists were determined to stand firm. The other colonists supported them. They believed that if Massachusetts gave way they too might lose their assemblies and have troops stationed in their towns.

The Continental Congress

In September 1774, representatives from twelve of the colonies met at a 'Continental Congress' in Philadelphia. They decided not to trade with Britain, and not to pay any taxes until the troops left Boston and the harbour was opened. They also agreed to prepare to defend themselves against British troops by training civilians to fight, and by hiding away stocks of guns.

The outbreak of war

The situation was very dangerous. In April 1775 Gage heard that colonists were storing arms at Concord near Boston. On the night of 18 April he sent a detachment of troops to seize the weapons. The soldiers were seen leaving Boston, and a colonist named Paul Revere rode out into the night to give the alarm in nearby villages.

As soon as they heard Revere's news, the men who made up the militia, as the new force was called, took their rifles and muskets and left their homes. They made their way in small groups to lie in wait along the road to Concord. As the troops approached they fired at them and then retreated into the night. The troops pressed on, reached Concord, destroyed a large quantity of arms and ammunition, and returned to Boston. But nearly 300 of them had been killed or wounded. The War of American Independence had begun.

▼ An American militiaman carried only his rifle, his ammunition and a little food

▲ British soldiers wore bright red tunics and white trousers

The rival forces

The British Army in America was a powerful force. British troops were well trained, and could be relied on to fight bravely. They were armed with smooth-bore muskets, which could fire a ball nearly 2 cm in diameter a distance of about 300 m, though they were only accurate up to 80 m. The men took about fifteen seconds to reload. At close quarters they relied on the bayonets on the end of their muskets to kill the enemy.

But the War in America did not suit the British Army. Many of the colonial militia were armed with rifles, which were much more accurate than muskets. A letter published in a British newspaper claimed that colonial riflemen 'could put a ball into a man's head' at 150 or 200 m. Only a very lucky shot from a musket would hit at that range. So the colonists kept their distance—within rifle-

shot, but out of range of muskets. If the British attacked, they retreated. These tactics annoyed the British. They complained that the Americans would not come out and fight.

Bunker Hill, 1775

During April and May 1775, the Massachusetts militia gradually surrounded Boston. In June they began to dig trenches on Bunker Hill, overlooking the harbour and the village of Charleston. It was an important position. General Howe, who had recently arrived from England, went with a force of 2,300 men to drive the militia away.

In a hard-fought battle the British troops struggled up the hill, stumbled through hay fields, and clambered over walls and fences. The militia, sheltering behind their newly-dug defences, kept up a deadly fire with muskets and rifles, and drove the British back twice. But when the weary troops attacked for a third time, the colonists were short of ammunition, and the British got to the top of the hill and charged the militia with their bayonets. The colonists fled, leaving 400 dead and wounded. The British had won, but they had suffered 1,054 casualties—226 of them killed.

Both sides were unhappy about the Battle of Bunker Hill. The colonists were angry that they had been driven from the hill, and the British were horrified by the number of their men wounded and killed. General Gage wrote, 'The loss we have sustained is greater than we can bear'. After Bunker Hill, Howe was always unwilling to attack the Americans if he thought they were well dug in.

Both sides now prepared for a long war. The colonists appointed George Washington as their commander-in-chief. He was a rich planter from Virginia who had fought against the French in the Seven Years War. He was honest, brave and determined. Under his orders the militia kept Boston surrounded. Howe could not break out, so in 1776 he sent for the Navy and they evacuated his troops from Boston.

Study 7

The War in America begins

1 Copy the time-chart opposite and use these words to fill in the spaces correctly:

Boston   ambush   casualties
weapons   troops

2 *Either*

(a) Draw the picture of the British soldier on page 18 and copy the caption.
(b) Why did the British troops' uniforms make them an easy target for the American militiamen?

Or

(a) Draw the picture of the American militiaman on page 18 and copy the caption.
(b) Why was there no need for the American militiamen at Concord to carry much food or clothing with them?

The War in America begins

Date	Event
April 1775	Am militiamen _____ Br troops sent to destroy _____ stored secretly at Concord.
May 1775	Br _____ capture Bunker Hill near _____ from the Am but suffer heavy _____ .

3(a) Copy the statements below.
At the Battle of Bunker Hill
the British troops struggled up the hill,
the Americans sheltered behind newly-dug defences,
the British won but they suffered 1,054 casualties.

(b) Now look at the picture of the battle on page 19. Which of the above statements does the picture show to be true? Give reasons for your answer.

The Declaration of Independence

In 1776 the leaders of the colonists took an important step. On 4 July they signed a document declaring that the Thirteen Colonies were now a free and independent country.

Many colonists, known as Loyalists, opposed the Declaration. They wanted the British Government to treat the colonies better, but they did not want to be independent. Most Loyalists waited to see how the struggle against Britain would turn out, but some helped the British forces. For instance, a few tried to organise bands of armed men to fight against the other colonists, but they were easily defeated.

The Declaration of Independence showed the British that if they lost the War, they would lose the colonies as well. So they decided to make a great effort to win, and sent Howe 20,000 fresh troops.

Howe at once attacked the Americans, and easily captured New York City and Long Island. Washington knew that trained British troops would easily beat his men in a pitched battle, so he retreated, drawing Howe after him. By the end of the year the British controlled the whole of the coast from Rhode Island to the River Delaware, but they had not defeated the American Army.

Study 8

What should the Loyalists do?

In groups of four:

1 Choose one of these parts each:

Jacob Fuller—aged 40
Luke Fuller—aged 20
Miriam Fuller—aged 38
Susan Fuller—aged 18

It is the autumn of 1776, and the British Army is advancing on the area in Connecticut where Jacob Fuller and his wife Miriam live, with their two children, Luke and Susan. The Fullers own a small farm. They are honest, self-reliant people who support the Loyalists. Most families in their area support the Declaration of Independence and several men have gone to fight in General Washington's army.

In your group:

2 Discuss
  (a) how each of you can help the British, for example, by giving them food and information,
  (b) how one person's actions may affect the rest of the family, for example, making the neighbouring families mistrust you because they suspect one of your family of being a British spy,
  (c) what may happen to the family when the British leave the area.
  Decide whether or not to help the British.

As a class:

3 Ask two groups to tell you what they have decided to do and why. Do the rest of you agree?

The defeat of the British

Saratoga, 1777

The turning-point of the War came in 1777. General Burgoyne, who commanded the British Army in Canada, decided to bring his forces south to help the British in New England. He expected Howe to come to meet him, but instead Howe advanced into Pennsylvania and captured Philadelphia. This left Burgoyne stranded at Saratoga, surrounded by colonial militiamen. As there was no sign of Howe, Burgoyne surrendered.

The surrender at Saratoga depressed the British generals. Howe told the Government he would need 80,000 men to defeat the Americans. The Government could not afford to send so many, and told Howe to keep his men on the coast, where they could stay in touch with the Navy. Howe did as he was told. But soon there was more bad news. When the French heard that Burgoyne had surrendered, they realised that they might be able to get their revenge for what they had suffered in the Seven Years War. So in 1778 they declared war, and sent troops and ships to help the colonists.

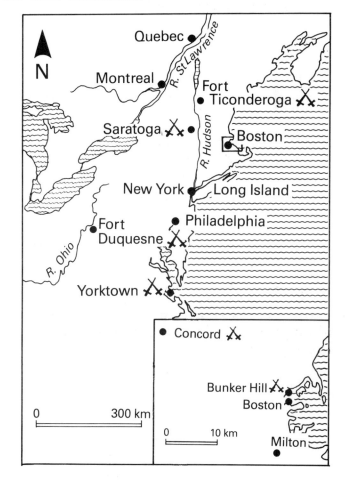

▶ The War of American Independence

21

▼ Cornwallis surrenders to George Washington, the
American commander, at Yorktown

The end of the War

The French Navy played a vital part in the defeat of the British. In 1781 General Cornwallis was stationed at Yorktown, a port on the coast of Virginia, with 70,000 British troops. A force of American and French troops besieged Yorktown, and Cornwallis had to rely on the Navy to supply him with food and ammunition. But in September, a French fleet arrived and blockaded the harbour. Cornwallis soon ran short of supplies, and in the middle of October he surrendered with his whole army.

The British Navy had lost control of the American coast. The fleet hit back quickly. In April 1782 British ships defeated the French at the Battle of the Saints in the West Indies. This made the coast of America safe for British ships once more. But it was too late.

Many MPs were now convinced that Britain would never defeat the colonists, and the Government decided to make peace. So in 1783, under the Treaty of Versailles, Britain gave up her claim to govern the Thirteen Colonies, and recognised them as the United States of America. Loyalists who did not want to stay in the United States went to Canada, which was still ruled by Britain, though many of the inhabitants were French.

Many people in Britain were very discouraged by the loss of the American colonies. They thought that British power in North America was at an end. They did not think that Canada was much use. Canadian furs were worth very little compared with Virginian tobacco. Indeed, some British politicians had wanted to exchange the whole of Canada for the small French island of Guadeloupe, which produced a valuable crop of sugar every year. Nobody at that time knew that Canada had huge reserves of valuable minerals under her soil.

Study 9

Independent Americans: loyal Canadians

1 Copy the time-chart opposite and fill in the gaps correctly.

2 (a) Why did the French enter the War after Burgoyne surrendered at Saratoga?
  (b) How did the French Army and Navy help the Americans capture Yorktown?

3 (a) Why did many Americans go to Canada after 1783?
  (b) Give an example to show that some people in Britain did not think that Canada was a very important part of the British Empire.

The War in America

Date	Event
1777	Saratoga. The _____ troops surrender to the _____ . The _____ declare war on Britain and help the colonists.
1781	Yorktown. The Americans and the _____ force the _____ to surrender.
1783	Treaty of Versailles. Britain agrees that the _____ States now form an independent country.

Further work

Writing

1 A *colony* is ruled by the country that the colonists first came from.
  A *state* is an independent country.
  (a) From which country did the colonists who lived in the Thirteen Colonies come?
  (b) Why did the colonists rename the colonies 'The United States of America' on 4 July 1776?

2 Before the War of Independence the citizens of Boston
    spoke English,
    accepted the British king as their king,
    went to church on Sundays,
    were used to seeing British soldiers in their streets,
    owned ships in the port and businesses in the city,
    had the reputation of being tough and self-confident.
  (a) Write brief notes saying which of the items listed above
    (i) would have changed as a result of the War of Independence,
    (ii) would not have changed.
    Give reasons for your answer.
  (b) Write two paragraphs under the heading 'Boston before and after the War of Independence'.

3 (a) Write brief notes on the reasons why many Americans
      welcomed the British Army before the Peace of Paris, 1763,
      disliked having the British Army in America after the Boston Tea Party, 1773,
      formed their own army to fight the British after the Battle of Bunker Hill, 1775.
  (b) Write three paragraphs under the heading 'The British Army in America, 1763 – 1775'.

Drawing

1 (a) Draw the picture of the Allyn House in Massachusetts on page 9.
  (b) Many New England houses that date from the eighteenth century are made of wood. What does this suggest about the kind of countryside the settlers found in this part of America?

→

23

→

2 (a) Draw a set of three pictures to illustrate the life of whites, black people and Indians in eighteenth-century America.
  (b) Write a caption under each picture, saying what it shows.

3 When the British troops surrendered at Yorktown their band played a tune called *The world turned upside down*. Draw a cartoon that might have appeared in a British newspaper in 1781, showing how the British felt ashamed and sad that the colonists they had once ruled were now giving the orders.

Figure it out

In the story of the Boston Tea Party we are told that
   the three ships at Griffin's Wharf each carried about 100 chests of tea,
   the 'Indians' took about three hours to unload the tea.

1 How many chests, on average, were unloaded from each ship in an hour?
2 How long, on average, did it take to unload each chest?
3 Do your answers to these questions confirm the statement on page 3 that unloading the chests was 'slow and difficult work'?

2 Sugar and slavery

Tacky's revolt

The new slaves

Zachary Bailey owned a sugar plantation in St Mary's parish on the island of Jamaica. In 1760 he and his neighbour, Ballard Beckford, bought a batch of just over 100 black slaves who had been imported from the Gold Coast in West Africa.

Both planters were pleased with their new slaves, who came from the Ashanti Kingdom. Ashanti people were famous for their strength and courage. They worked very hard, and could endure pain and fatigue without complaining. So they made good slaves.

Bailey took his new slaves to the huts where they were to live, gave them rough linen clothes to wear, and issued each of them with a knife for cutting the sugar cane. Then he left to visit a friend who lived a few miles away in Ballard's Valley.

Tacky and the obeah men

One of Beckford's new slaves was a man named Tacky. In Africa he had been a headman in his village, and he was determined not to live as a slave in Jamaica. He found that many of the Ashanti agreed with him. So he began to organise a rebellion.

Among the Ashanti slaves there were several witch doctors, known as *obeah men*. They made magic using dust gathered from graveyards, birds' bones, feathers, eggshells, dogs' teeth and blood. They made charms to keep away evil spirits. They provided medicines to cure the sick, and gave people poisons to kill their enemies. They encouraged Tacky and his friends. One of them gave the rebels a special powder. He said that if they rubbed it on their bodies they would be safe from all harm.

The revolt begins

At dead of night Tacky and his men left Beckford's plantation and made their way to Bailey's, where they easily persuaded more Ashanti men to join them. The rebels now numbered well over 100. Guided by a slave who knew the island well, they made for a fort at Port

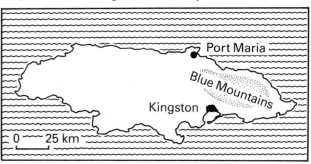

▼ Jamaica in the eighteenth century

Maria. They found one sentry on guard. They killed him, broke into the fort, and took guns and ammunition.

The armed Ashanti then went to Ballard's Valley. Bailey, who was still there, went out to meet them. He saw them coming up the valley, waving their guns and shouting Ashanti war cries. He tried to approach them, but they shot at him. So he slipped away to get help from neighbouring plantations.

The defeat of the slaves

While Bailey was away Tacky's men broke into the overseer's house in Ballard's Valley, killed the overseer and his family, and set fire to the house. When Bailey returned with a force of 130 armed men, he found the Ashanti roasting an ox in front of the blazing building and drinking rum they had taken from the house. Bailey's men attacked. They killed eight or nine rebels, and wounded several more. The rest, including Tacky, fled into the woods.

A party of soldiers were sent from Kingston, the capital of Jamaica, to hunt down the Ashanti. The soldiers were helped by a number of maroons—descendants of slaves kept by the Spaniards before the English captured Jamaica in 1656.

The rebels scatter

One party of troops and maroons made their way into the hills to hunt for rebels. At night they camped in a clearing and lit a fire. A party of rebels armed with muskets attacked the camp. The soldiers, illuminated by the flames of the fire, made perfect targets, while the rebels were hidden in the darkness. Many soldiers were killed, but the rest fought back, firing at the flash of the rebels' musket-shots in the woods.

Eventually the rebels crept away, leaving several dead men behind them, and the next day the troops again went out to search for them. But the Ashanti had scattered, and only a few were captured. The rest tried to survive by hunting in the hills. One day a party of maroons saw Tacky, alone and unarmed. He tried to run away, but they chased him, and when they got near enough they shot him dead.

The punishment of the rebels

One of the wounded Ashanti who was captured was angry that the obeah man's powder had not protected him. So he told the authorities how the obeah man had encouraged them all to rebel. The obeah man was arrested, and was sentenced to be hanged. He did not care. He said that his magic was so powerful that the white men would not be able to harm him. He was hanged in public in Kingston. When he died, many of the slaves present were very surprised that his magic had not protected him.

Three captured Ashanti rebels, who had helped to kill the overseer and his family in Ballard's Valley, were also executed. One was slowly burnt to death. He suffered in silence. The other two were hung up alive in chains in Kingston Square and left to die. They lived for more than a week. They never complained, or showed any sign of pain. In fact they spent much of the time laughing and joking with onlookers. The Ashanti rebels believed it was better to die bravely than to live as slaves.

Study 1

How do we know?

Bryan Edwards's book

In 1760 Bryan Edwards—a relative of Zachary Bailey—was in Jamaica, learning how to run a sugar plantation. Bailey was good to the young man and helped him as much as he could. Thirty years later, Bryan Edwards wrote a book about the West Indies and described what had happened there at the time of Tacky's revolt. He said that the slaves had no excuse for turning against their masters. Zachary Bailey always treated them well and so did his overseer, Andrew Fletcher. The Ashanti could have killed Fletcher, but they spared his life because they did not think he deserved to die.

Before the revolt, Bryan Edwards talked to some of the Ashanti about their life in Africa. They told him about the wars between the African nations and how the people who were defeated were made slaves. Some of the Ashanti said that they had been born free, and when Bryan Edwards asked their relatives among the slaves if this was true, they agreed that it was. He decided that some of the Ashanti may even have owned slaves themselves when they lived in Africa, and fought with other Africans.

1 (a) Where was Bryan Edwards at the time of Tacky's revolt?
  (b) Would you expect him to remember the events of the revolt clearly when he wrote his book thirty years later? Give reasons for your answer.
2 Bryan Edwards says that his relative, Zachary Bailey, was a good master. Why does what he tells us about the Ashanti and Andrew Fletcher help to confirm this statement?
3 What did Bryan Edwards do that shows that
  (a) he was interested in the Ashanti,
  (b) he tried to check the information they gave him?

What do you think?

If we say that someone is *biased*, we mean that he or she takes it for granted that one side in a quarrel or argument is right, and does not consider the other side's point of view. Consider Bryan Edwards's connection with Bailey, his conversations with the Ashanti, and what he says about the slaves who rebelled. Do you think he was biased? Give reasons for your answer.

Study 2

The forts on the Gold Coast

In 1839 a group of British people who were trying to stop the slave trade visited the Gold Coast of Africa, which by that time was controlled by the British. The British had freed all the slaves in their Empire and had banned the slave trade, but slaves were still being exported from some parts of Africa to the plantations of the United States.

The British visitors were shown the ruins of some old forts. The British governor said the slave-traders had once used the forts as great storehouses for cargoes of slaves waiting to be shipped across the Atlantic.

1 The story of Tacky's revolt says that the Ashanti slaves came from the Gold Coast.
   (a) What ruins did the British visitors see on the Gold Coast?
   (b) Who told them that the forts were connected with the slave trade?

2 The story says that Beckford purchased Tacky in a cargo of 100 slaves. Which word in the governor's statement (opposite) suggests that the slave-traders could assemble large numbers of slaves in the forts?

3 We are told in the story that Tacky was sent to the West Indies in about 1760.
   (a) In what year did the visitors to the Gold Coast see the forts?
   (b) The forts were in ruins. Does this mean that they could not have been in use when Tacky was alive? Give reasons for your answer.

What do you think?
Which of these statements do you think is more accurate?
> The forts on the Gold Coast give us useful information about the slave trade at the time of Tacky's revolt.
> The forts on the Gold Coast are evidence that Tacky's revolt took place.

Give reasons for your answer.

Understanding what happened

1 List these events in the order in which they happened:

> Bailey gets help from neighbouring plantations.
> The rebels attack the soldiers' camp, but are driven off and scattered.
> Tacky and the slaves from Beckford's and Bailey's plantations capture weapons from Port Maria and march on Ballard's Valley.
> Tacky is killed and the captured Ashanti are executed.
> The Ashanti slaves arrive in Jamaica.
> The slaves are driven into the woods and are hunted by soldiers and maroons.

2 (a) Why were the Ashanti
   (i) willing to accept Tacky as their leader,
   (ii) convinced that their rebellion would be successful?

   (b) Give an example of something that the Ashanti did that would have made their masters
   (i) fear them,
   (ii) respect them,
   (iii) think that they were ignorant savages.

   (c) The maroons were descended from slaves. Why may they have decided to help the plantation owners and not the rebel Ashanti?

3 (a) What are we told in the story that suggests that Bailey did not expect his slaves to rebel?

   (b) Does the story give the impression that
   > the slaves outnumbered the white people in Jamaica,
   > the white people outnumbered the slaves in Jamaica?
   Give reasons for your answer.

   (c) The rebels who were captured died slowly and in great pain. What reasons may the plantation owners have had for treating them so cruelly?

Further work

Writing

1 Write an account of the slaves' attack on the soldiers' camp in the hills from the point of view of *either* a slave *or* a soldier.

2 Write *two* accounts of the attack on Ballard's Valley, one from Tacky's point of view and one from Zachary Bailey's.

3 Write an article that might have appeared in a British newspaper in 1761, reporting the death of Tacky. Remind the readers, briefly, why the soldiers are hunting for Tacky and why the Jamaican planters will be pleased to know that he is dead.

Drawing

1 Draw the map of the West Indies on page 29. Write two sentences saying on which island
   slaves rebelled unsuccessfully in 1760,
   slaves rebelled successfully in 1791.

2 (a) Draw the map of Jamaica below.
   (b) Annotate your map to show what happened at each of these places:

   Port Maria
   Ballard's Valley   Kingston

   For example, you might show Kingston as follows:

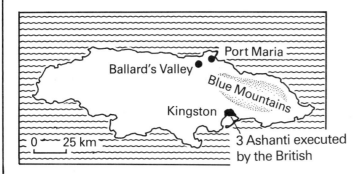

3 (a) Draw six pictures telling Tacky's life story, as you think it probably happened, from the time when he was a headman in an African village, to his death in Jamaica.
   (b) Write a brief caption under each picture.

Drama

In groups of three:

1 Write a scene showing the Ashanti planning their revolt on Beckford's plantation. The meeting breaks up when they hear the overseer approaching. Choose one of these parts each:
   the obeah man—who promises his magic will protect the rebels,
   Tacky—who, as a headman, will lead the rebels,
   an Ashanti slave—who is uncertain if it is wise to rebel.

   Give each person at least four things to say.

2 Rehearse your scenes in your groups.

3 Choose two groups to perform their scenes to the class.

Glossary

Add the words below to your glossary and explain, in your own words, what each of them means:

   maroon   overseer   obeah man

The sugar industry

The sugar islands

At the end of the eighteenth century Britain had a number of colonies in the West Indies. Most of them had been captured from France or Spain. Their main product was sugar, which they exported to Britain in cargo ships known as 'West Indiamen'. The demand for sugar was constantly increasing in Britain as the population grew and became more prosperous.

Making sugar

West Indian sugar came from sugar cane which was grown on large plantations. Labourers on a sugar plantation had to work hard. To grow well, the cane needed a rich, deep soil, so they had to dig and manure the ground thoroughly. Then they planted cuttings of cane. As the cane grew, they had to weed it and check it regularly to make sure that it was clean and free from disease.

After eighteen months the cane was fully grown. It was usually about 2 m high, with a plume of leaves growing out of the top. When it was ripe the cane turned yellow, and was about 2 cm in diameter. Then the labourers cut it down and trimmed off the leaves. Cutting was hard and dangerous work, for the cane was tough, and its leaves had sharp edges which could inflict deep cuts.

Next the labourers carried the heavy canes to a mill, where the stems were crushed between two heavy rollers to squeeze the sugary sap out of them. Usually horses or donkeys worked the mill, but some were powered by water-wheels.

The sugary syrup was piped from the mill to the boiling-room. Here it was heated in huge coppers and boiled to get rid of the surplus liquid. As the syrup boiled, a sticky scum rose to the surface. This had to be skimmed off, as it contained impurities which would spoil the sugar. The boiling-room was always hot and humid. It was hard work skimming the sugar and keeping the fires stoked. Dried sugar cane was used as fuel, and it burnt away very quickly.

Usually the sugar was boiled several times. Eventually, when it was thick and treacly, it was left to cool. Gradually the liquid separated. Brown sugar crystals formed on the top. Underneath there was a thick, brown, sweet liquid known as molasses. The molasses were drained off and used to make rum. The sugar was packed into barrels and shipped to refineries in Britain to be made into white sugar and sold.

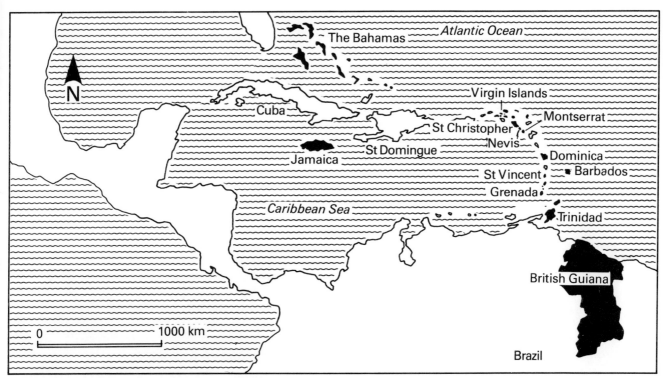

▲ The West Indies in the eighteenth century. British colonies are shaded in black. Tacky's revolt on Jamaica in 1760 failed. Slaves who rebelled in the French colony of St Domingue in 1791 won their independence

▼ The slaves are preparing this ground for the cane to be planted

Labour problems

British planters who had settled in the West Indies easily sold all the sugar they produced. But they found it difficult to get people to work for them.

Workers

In the seventeenth century the planters organised a scheme for 'servants' to come out from Britain to work for four years on the plantations. The servants were promised a piece of land where at the end of this time they could set up as planters. The scheme did not work. Planters treated their servants badly. They made them work long hours and gave them poor food. A petition from Barbados complained that servants spent their time 'grinding at the mills and attending the

▲ Inside a boiling-room in Antigua. (A nineteenth-century engraving)

furnaces, or digging in this scorching island having nothing to feed on but potato roots, nor to drink but water, and sleeping in sties worse than hogs in England'. In the hot climate many died. Most of the survivors found that at the end of their four years there was no land for them. Instead they were given just over 100 kg of sugar, worth less than £2.

Convicts and kidnappers

Very few people were willing to go to the West Indies to work as servants. But the planters had to find labourers. So the Government sent them convicts and prisoners of war. Oliver Cromwell sent men captured in wars against Scotland and Ireland. James II sent out men from Dorset and Somerset who had rebelled against him in 1685. Criminals sentenced to death for stealing were reprieved, and sent to work for ten years in the plantations instead. Planters found that most convicts were lazy and careless, so they flogged them to make them work harder.

The population of the main islands of the British West Indies in 1791

	Black	White
Jamaica	250,000	30,000
Barbados	62,115	16,167
Grenada	23,926	1,000
St Vincent	11,853	1,450
Dominica	14,967	1,236

There were still not enough workers on the plantations, so some planters paid sea-captains to kidnap innocent victims in Britain, and ship them to the West Indies. In Bristol local merchants organised a trade in the children of poor families. Men and women enticed the children away with sweets, and put them on board ships bound for the sugar islands. Most merchants thought there was nothing wrong with kidnapping. They had a shock in 1685 when Lord Chief Justice Jeffreys, who was in Bristol to try criminal cases, suddenly ordered the Lord Mayor to go into the dock, called him 'a kidnapping villain', threatened to cut off his ears, and fined him £1,000.

Study 3

White workers in the West Indies

1 (a) Write a sentence about each of the stages of sugar production listed below, saying why it was hard work for the labourers:

  planting sugar,
  cutting sugar,
  boiling sugar.

  (b) The West Indies exported rum and brown sugar. Which of these exports
   (i) was a finished product when it left the West Indies,
   (ii) provided jobs in Britain for workers who carried out the next stage of production?

2 (a) List five types of white people who worked on the West Indian sugar plantations.

  (b) Which group of people
   (i) knew they would never see Britain again,
   (ii) hoped to return to Britain after ten years,
   (iii) were promised land in return for their labour but only received 100 kg of sugar?

3 (a) Copy the population table of the main British West Indian islands in 1791, above.

  (b) Of the five islands listed, what was the total
   (i) of the black population,
   (ii) of the white population?

  (c) Roughly how many black people were there in Jamaica for every white person?

Slavery in the islands

Some planters in the seventeenth century had black slaves from Africa working on their plantations. These planters prospered, and soon others began to buy slaves.

Slave cabins

Most slaves led a wretched life. On many plantations they slept in wattle-and-plaster cabins about 3 m long. The floor was earth, and the roof was made of palm leaves. The cabins were low and dark, and had no windows. They were divided into two rooms. In one room there was a bedstead with a mat and a blanket. In the other there were a rough table, some stools, a few earthenware jars for storing food, an iron cooking-pot, and some calabash shells which were used as plates and cups. At night the slaves lit a fire in the middle of one of the rooms to keep the cabin warm, and the smoke drifted out through the roof or the door opening.

The work of a slave

Six days a week, just before dawn, the slaves were woken by the sound of a bell or a blast on a horn. They had to get up quickly and line up outside carrying their tools and their breakfast. Overseers with whips beat any who arrived late, and then marched them all off to the sugar fields. At about six o'clock, as dawn broke, the slaves began their work.

The youngest and weakest weeded the sugar cane, carefully pulling out every blade of grass. Stronger slaves worked in rows, digging the ground and dividing it up into squares ready for planting, while others planted the cane shoots. At harvest-time they were all busy cutting and carrying the cane. All the time, overseers carrying whips watched them and hit any slaves who were working slowly or carelessly. If a slave dared to complain he was flogged mercilessly, and if he struck an overseer he was hanged.

At nine o'clock the slaves had a break of three-quarters of an hour for breakfast. At twelve they were given lunch. This usually consisted of mushy beans and dried fish. After lunch the slaves rested through the heat of the day until two o'clock. Then they started work again and went on until sunset—about six o'clock. They gathered up their tools and marched back to their cabins, where they prepared their own evening meals and then lay down to rest until morning.

▲ Slaves cutting the cane at harvest-time. (An engraving made in 1823)

Slaves who worked in the boiling-rooms were usually worse off than those who laboured in the fields. The heat and steam made them ill. Their legs and faces swelled. Some collapsed and died. Others became so drowsy that they were careless, and burnt themselves with boiling sugar.

A few slaves worked for the planters and overseers as domestic servants. They cooked, cleaned and waited on their masters and mistresses. Some who worked as nursemaids, ladies' maids and valets got to know their owners very well, and became trusted members of the household. They were properly fed and well clothed. But if they upset any of the family, they might well be beaten and sent out to work on the plantation or in the boiling-room.

Gardens and markets

Most slaves were given a small piece of ground on which they grew fruit and vegetables. They also kept pigs, goats and chickens. They needed the extra food provided in this way because it was impossible to keep healthy on the diet provided by the plantation owners. At harvest-time they got extra nourishment by chewing the ripe sugar cane. Most owners did not mind this because the sugar syrup gave the slaves extra energy and they

were able to work harder. But a few planters thought it was a waste of cane, and made their slaves wear gags which stopped them chewing while they were at work.

On Sundays the slaves had a day off. They spent it working in their gardens, making ropes out of tree-bark, or weaving baskets from dried cane shoots and leaves. In some areas there were markets on Sundays where the slaves could sell or exchange their goods.

Working animals

Most planters did not think of their slaves as human beings. They thought of them as working animals, like horses or donkeys. Planters found it difficult to decide how to treat their slaves. Some said it was better to give them good food and dry cabins and allow them plenty of rest because they would live longer, and have children. This meant that the planters would not have to buy as many new slaves. Others said it was cheaper in the long run to make the slaves work very hard, and spend very little on their food and lodging. The slaves would only live about eight years, but replacements would cost less than the extra food and drink needed to keep the others alive for longer.

Working from dawn to dusk

1 (a) Draw the picture of slaves and their cabins on page 33.
   (b) Read the section headed 'Slave cabins' on page 32.
   (c) Write brief notes on (i) lighting and heating in a slave's cabin, (ii) the cabin's furniture.
2 (a) Read the section headed 'The work of a slave' on page 32.
   (b) Copy the timetable below.
   (c) Complete the timetable to show
      (i) when a slave was working or resting,
      (ii) other information about his work or the food he ate during a break.

(d) Which types of work were
   (i) better than field work,
   (ii) worse than field work?
   Give reasons for your answer.
3 (a) Read the sections headed 'Gardens and markets' and 'Working animals' on page 33.
   (b) Explain
      (i) how a plantation owner could reward or punish his slaves by moving them to a different type of work,
      (ii) why many slaves died after working in the West Indies for about eight years.

A slave's day

Time	Work or break	Other information
6.00 a.m. – 9.00 a.m.	_____	_____
9.00 a.m. – 9.45 a.m.	_____	_____
9.45 a.m. – 12 noon	_____	_____
12 noon – 2.00 p.m.	_____	_____
2.00 p.m. – 6.00 p.m.	_____	_____

The slave trade

The Triangular Trade

African slaves were taken to the West Indies in British ships, which carried on a three-cornered or 'triangular' trade. Ships set out from Britain loaded with cloth, iron bars, tools, guns and beads, and sailed to the west coast of Africa, where slave merchants had cargoes of slaves waiting for them. Then, in the 'middle passage', the slaves were taken to the West Indies where they were sold. Finally the ships returned to Britain to pick up more goods.

Buying slaves

As soon as a ship reached the African coast, the captain went ashore, to exchange the goods he had brought from England for a cargo of slaves. He examined the slaves carefully, and tried to pick a shipload of fit young men and women—though usually the merchant made him take some

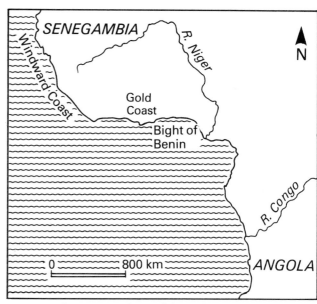

▲ Most slaves were shipped from this part of the African coast

▼ Slaves being loaded on board ship. (A nineteenth-century print)

old, weak slaves as well. When the captain had chosen his slaves, his mark was branded on them with a hot iron. This prevented the merchant replacing them with inferior slaves while the captain's back was turned.

Most slave merchants on the coast were Africans. White men who tried to set up in business often died of malaria, or some other tropical disease. Indeed, so many Europeans died there that it was known as 'the white man's grave'.

The African merchants bought slaves from various sources. Some were captured in wars between tribes. Some had been kidnapped. Some had borrowed money, had been unable to pay it back, and had been sold to pay off their debts. Others were criminals, sentenced to be sold into slavery for robbery, assault or even murder.

The slave trade in 1771

British ports from which slave ships sailed

Port	No. of ships	Slaves carried
Liverpool	107	29,250
London	58	8,136
Bristol	23	8,810
Lancaster	4	950

African ports where slaves were bought

Ports called at	No. of ships	Slaves bought
Senegambia	40	3,310
Windward Coast	56	11,960
Gold Coast	29	7,525
Bight of Benin	63	23,301
Angola	4	1,050

When the captain had chosen all the slaves he wanted, he and the merchant went on board ship and bargained until they agreed how many bars of iron, tools, or rolls of cloth the slaves were worth. The merchant checked the goods as carefully as the captain had examined the slaves. He could tell how much a roll of cloth or a batch of knife-blades was worth. Eventually the two men agreed their bargain and sealed it with a drink of rum. The slaves were brought on board, and the goods were taken ashore and put in the merchant's warehouse.

The middle passage

The crew of the ship chained the slaves together in pairs, and forced them down a ladder into a hold below the main deck. Usually the hold was not high enough for a man or woman to stand upright, and so many slaves were crammed into it that they hardly had enough room to lie down.

The only air came in through gratings in the deck. There was very little light, and the air was so foul and short of oxygen that one surgeon found that the flame of his candle went out when he went down onto the slave deck.

On most ships, the slave decks were washed down with buckets of sea-water every few days, but even so they stank, and when the weather was hot the atmosphere was almost unbearable. Richard Drake, an American trader, carried a bag of camphor clenched between his teeth to try to counteract the 'hideous stench' when he went below to check on his slaves.

It was very unhealthy between decks, and the slaves were brought up on deck a few at a time for exercise and fresh air. One of the crew beat a drum, and the slaves had to dance in time to it. Another member of the crew stood by with a whip to beat them if they danced too slowly. Some captains also made the slaves sing. After a few minutes on deck, the slaves were forced back down below, and a few more were brought out. This continued until all the slaves had been on deck for exercise.

In wet and stormy weather the crew covered the gratings to keep the rain and the sea out. The slaves were left in total darkness until the weather improved. Some were seasick, and infectious diseases spread quickly in the confined space. Alexander Falconbridge, a ship's surgeon, described how he went below after 'some wet and blowing weather', and discovered the floor covered with blood and filth. Many slaves had fainted. They were carried up on deck where several died. Another surgeon recalled that he once found a woman slave, chained to a dead body, giving birth to a baby. Traders expected some slaves to die on the voyage—perhaps up to a quarter of the total. But sometimes smallpox or dysentery broke out on the ship, and as many as half the slaves might die.

Occasionally slaves mutinied and tried to take over a ship. On one voyage they struck off their irons on an anchor stowed between decks. Then they forced open the gratings and scrambled up onto the deck. One of the crew gave the alarm, and the rest seized guns and opened fire. They shot twenty slaves dead. The rest jumped back below.

The crew of a slave ship were always on the lookout for troublemakers during the voyage. If slaves were disobedient or impertinent they were punished. Some had their thumbs crushed with thumbscrews. Some were cruelly whipped. Others were weighed down with heavy chains or forced to wear tight iron collars.

The end of the voyage

After about two months at sea, the slave ship neared the West Indies. Conditions for the slaves improved. For most of the voyage they had been fed on a scanty diet of porridge made of ground Indian corn flavoured with salt, pepper and palm oil. Now they were also given beans and dried fish. Any slave who refused to eat had his mouth forced open by an iron gag and food thrust down his throat. When they neared the shore the crew struck off their irons and gave them oil to rub over their bodies until they gleamed. Those with grey hair had it washed with dye until it looked black. All this was to make the slaves look young and healthy so that they would fetch a better price.

When the ship dropped anchor everybody on board was relieved. The crew were delighted to be going ashore to enjoy themselves in the nearby taverns, while the slaves could at least look forward to leaving the dark, filthy hold where they had spent the last two months. Usually the owner of the ship had an agent in the West Indies. The captain handed the slaves over to the agent to sell, and his crew set to work cleaning and disinfecting the ship with vinegar and water. Then he set sail for England.

The profits of the trade

When he reached his home port, the captain was ready to pick up his cargo of iron, cloth, tools and beads and sail to Africa to collect more slaves.

The Triangular Trade could be very profitable, especially if the slaves remained fit and well. In 1720 the *King Solomon* set sail from Britain with cargo that had cost £4,252. In Africa the captain exchanged it for 296 black slaves, and sold them in the West Indies for £9,228. Even allowing for food, water and the wages of the crew, he made a handsome profit. But the slave trade was very risky. If a large number of slaves died there might not be enough left to make a profit when they were sold. Often captains overloaded their ships, and some sank without trace in tropical storms. Over the years slave-traders probably made an average profit of about ten per cent.

TO BE SOLD & LET
BY PUBLIC AUCTION,
On MONDAY the 18th of MAY, 1829,
UNDER THE TREES.

FOR SALE,
THE THREE FOLLOWING
SLAVES,
VIZ.

HANNIBAL, about 30 Years old, an excellent House Servant, of Good Character.
WILLIAM, about 35 Years old, a Labourer.
NANCY, an excellent House Servant and Nurse.
The MEN belonging to "LEECH'S" Estate, and the WOMAN to Mrs. D. SMIT

TO BE LET,
On the usual conditions of the Hirer finding them in Food, Clothe and Medical
THE FOLLOWING
MALE and FEMALE
SLAVES,
OF GOOD CHARACTERS,

ROBERT BAGLEY, about 20 Years old, a good House Servant.
WILLIAM BAGLEY, about 18 Years old, a Labourer.
JOHN ARMS, about 18 Years old.
JACK ANTONIA, about 40 Years old, a Labourer.
PHILIP, an Excellent Fisherman.
HARRY, about 27 Years old, a good House Servant.
LUCY, a Young Woman of good Character, used to House Work and the Nursery.
ELIZA, an Excellent Washerwoman.
CLARA, an Excellent Washerwoman.
FANNY, about 14 Years old, House Servant.
SARAH, about 14 Years old, House Servant.

Also for Sale, at Eleven o'Clock,
Fine Rice, Gram, Paddy, Books, Muslins, Needles, Pins, Ribbons &c. &c.

AT ONE O'CLOCK, THAT CELEBRATED ENGLISH HORSE
BLUCHER,

Study 5

Slave-trading

1 (a) The notes below describe the work of three types of men who were connected with the slave trade. Copy them into your books:

Carried Br cloth and iron goods to W Afr.	Traded for slvs from various sources.	Lived in W Indies.
Traded Br goods for W Afr slvs.	Sold slvs to white traders.	Auctioned new slvs.
Carried slvs to W Indies.		

(b) Read the section headed 'The slave trade' on pages 34 to 37, and write each of these names under the correct list:
  British agent British captain
        African merchant

(c) Using the abbreviation ∴ write notes explaining how buying and selling slaves formed part of the Triangular Trade.

2 (a) Copy the map below.
(b) Look at the key to the map.
  (i) How many slaves are shown leaving Africa?
  (ii) Imagine that 50 slaves died on the voyage. Draw symbols on your map to show the number of slaves who were unloaded in the West Indies.

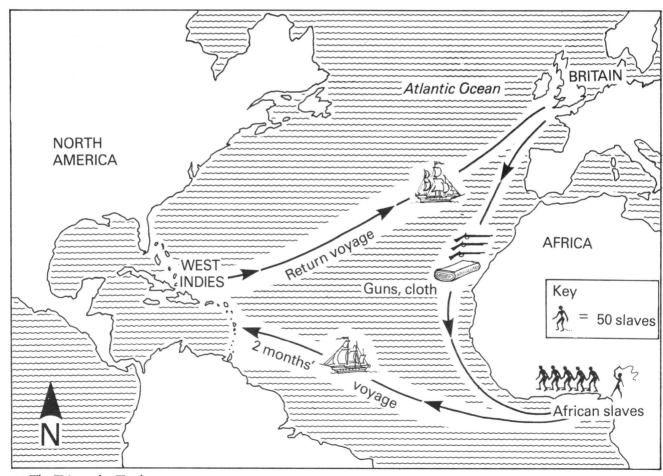

▲ The Triangular Trade

(c) Using the abbreviation `∴` write brief notes explaining why
  (i) up to half the slaves might die on the voyage,
  (ii) slaves were treated better towards the end of the voyage.

3 (a) Look at the table showing British ports from which slave ships sailed in 1771, on page 35. What was the total number
  (i) of British ships in the slave trade,
  (ii) of slaves carried by these ships?

(b) Roughly what percentage of slave ships came from Liverpool?

(c) Using the abbreviation `∴` write notes explaining why a slave-trader's profits averaged out at about ten per cent over a number of years.

4 Use your notes to write a paragraph on one or more of the following:
  British and African slave-traders,
  A slave's voyage to the West Indies,
  Liverpool and the slave trade.

Slavery and industry

Important changes were taking place in British society during the eighteenth century. The population was increasing fast, and new industries using power-driven machinery were beginning to produce huge quantities of cheap cloth, coal and iron.

The slave trade helped some of the new industries to develop. Some merchants who made money out of the trade built factories in Britain. Slave-traders bought large quantities of cloth from British manufacturers. They exchanged some of this for slaves in Africa, and sold some of it to plantation owners for the slaves to wear. The slave-traders also bought various sorts of ironware—bars and tools to trade for slaves in Africa, hoops for sugar barrels, knives and cooking-pots to take to the plantations, and even

handcuffs, gags and leg-irons to restrain the slaves on the voyage. In addition, sugar refiners, rum distillers, boatbuilders and sailors all depended on the slaves for a living.

Rich and powerful people living in Britain owned plantations and slaves in the West Indies. For instance, Lord Liverpool, Lord Chandos and the Earl of Crawford all owned slaves. So did William Beckford, a rich merchant who was Lord Mayor of London twice. John Gladstone, a Liverpool businessman, owned a valuable slave plantation in British Guiana. The Bishop of Exeter owned slaves, and so did the Society for the Propagation of the Gospel, a Christian missionary group. It branded its slaves with the word 'Society' to distinguish them from those belonging to other owners.

▲ Fonthill Abbey, in Wiltshire, was built for William Beckford's son. It was paid for with profits made from the sugar and slave trades

Study 6

Britain and the slave trade

1 A merchant or a plantation owner who made money from the slave trade might have spent it on a factory, or a country house.
Give an example of
(a) how the owner of the factory might have used the cloth made in it in the slave trade,
(b) a country house that was built by a plantation owner.

2 British workers in the eighteenth century often depended on the slave trade for their living.
Give an example of
(a) iron goods made in Britain that were used in the slave trade or on plantations,
(b) goods produced in the West Indies that were refined or distilled by workers in Britain.

3 Important officials were not ashamed to own slaves.
(a) Give an example of
(i) a lord mayor who owned slaves,
(ii) a bishop who owned slaves.
(b) How do we know that, at this time, the Society for the Propagation of the Gospel was not ashamed to own slaves?

▶ A working man and woman of about 1830

Study 7

The Lancashire cotton trade

Most of the cotton goods that were traded for slaves or used on the plantations in the West Indies were made in Lancashire, in factories in and around Manchester. The ships that brought the raw cotton docked at Liverpool, unloaded their cargoes and collected bales of woven cloth. Porters loaded the raw cotton onto packhorses and it was taken over rough roads to the factories.

In 1759 the Duke of Bridgewater hired James Brindley to build a canal to carry coal from his mines in Worsley to Manchester. Brindley was a skilful engineer and he built an aqueduct to carry the canal over the River Irwell. The canal was named the Bridgewater Canal. The Duke was so pleased with Brindley's work that he asked him to

cut an extension to the canal, linking Manchester with the Mersey Estuary. Gangs of labourers called *navigators* or *navvies* shifted tons of earth with their picks and shovels to cut the bed of the canal. When it was completed in 1773, the barges on the Bridgewater Canal carried cotton to and from Manchester more quickly than the teams of packhorses. The cotton manufacturers now found that it cost them 6 shillings to have a tonne of cotton delivered to Liverpool instead of £2. This meant that they could expand their trade and large quantities of cotton goods were exported to Europe and other countries overseas. The profits from the cotton industry helped to make Liverpool and Manchester two of the richest cities in Britain.

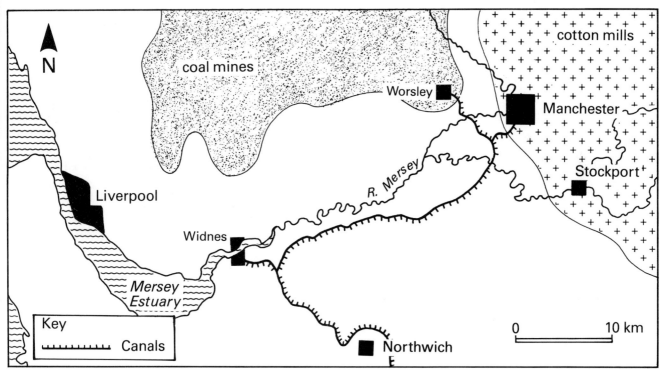

▲ Canals and industries in the Liverpool – Manchester region, 1773

1 Copy the map of the Liverpool – Manchester region above.

2 On your map name
    the River Irwell,
    the extension of the Bridgewater Canal.

3 Write 'A' on your map at the point where Brindley built an aqueduct.
4 Roughly how long, in kilometres, are the sections of the Bridgewater Canal that run from
    Worsley to Manchester,
    Manchester to Widnes?

→

Writing

1 Write one or two sentences saying what kind of goods were carried along the Bridgewater Canal.
2 Write a paragraph of three or four sentences under the heading 'Navvies'.
Mention:
> why they were called navvies,
> the kind of work they did,
> why there was plenty of work for them in the Liverpool – Manchester region between 1759 and 1773.

3 Write a paragraph of four or five sentences showing how the work of James Brindley helped Liverpool and Manchester to become prosperous cities.
Mention:
> why the first part of the Bridgewater Canal was built,
> the goods that the canal carried when it was extended,
> how the canal helped the manufacturers to increase their profits.

The fight against slavery

Arguments in favour of slavery

Most Europeans in the eighteenth century thought there was nothing wrong with slavery. They pointed out that the ancient Greeks and Romans had kept slaves, and that there was nothing in the Bible to say that slavery was wrong. Christian missionaries in the West Indies owned slaves, and clergymen in Bristol ordered the church bells to be rung when Parliament defeated a Bill to abolish the slave trade.

Many white planters did not think there was anything wrong in owning slaves because, they said, black people belonged to a different species. They said that African women could give birth without feeling any pain, and that a black person's senses of touch and taste were not as sensitive as those of white people. Bryan Edwards, the Jamaican planter, even wrote that black men and women could never form long-lasting relationships with each other. Many white people believed this kind of thing because they did not know any better.

The law regarded slaves as no better than animals. In 1783 the *Zong*, a slave ship, ran short of water on its voyage across the Atlantic. To conserve supplies, the captain ordered the crew to throw 130 slaves overboard. Nobody thought of accusing him of murder. Instead the owners of the ship claimed compensation from their insurance company for the loss of the slaves. They said that running short of water was 'a peril of the sea' which was covered by their policy. Lord Chief Justice Mansfield agreed with them. He said it was 'the same as if horses had been thrown overboard', and awarded the owners £30 per slave in compensation.

West Indian planters also argued that their slaves were much better off than they would have been if they had stayed in Africa. They said that most slaves put up for sale were either criminals or prisoners of war, who would have been killed or become slaves in Africa if they had not been sold to the slave-dealers. James Boswell, a Scottish lawyer, maintained that slavery on the sugar plantations saved Africans from 'massacre or intolerable bondage in their own country', and was 'a much happier state of life'. Bryan Edwards wrote that one of his slaves agreed with Boswell. The slave said that life in Jamaica was better than in her own country, Guinea, because 'people were not killed as in Guinea at the funeral of their masters'. Certainly, in some parts of Africa, wives

▲ A slave being branded. (A nineteenth-century print)

and slaves were killed when a chief died, but the planters pretended that human sacrifice often took place in Africa. This was not true.

The planters and their friends always boasted that they treated their slaves well. They said that slaves were better housed than many workers in Britain, and worked about the same hours. They also said that the punishments that the slaves suffered—such as flogging—were no worse than those given to British soldiers and sailors.

Planters and traders also said that slavery was necessary for Britain and the colonies to prosper. A Liverpool writer pointed out that 'it was the capital made in the African slave trade that built some of our docks', and in 1790 it was said that Liverpool would be ruined if the slave trade was abolished. In 1792, the Assembly of Jamaica declared that the safety of the West Indies depended on the slave trade. Some British admirals even said that many sailors in the Navy had learnt their trade sailing on slave ships. They were afraid that if slavery was abolished they would not be able to find enough sailors to man the king's ships.

The Abolitionists

But even in the eighteenth century, there were some people who believed that it was wrong for one human being to own another. In 1787, twelve of them formed an anti-slave trade committee. They found out as much as they could about

▼ In 1791 Toussaint L'Ouverture led a successful slave revolt on the French island of St Domingue, which became an independent country. The new Government changed the country's name to Haiti

▲ Slaves in Jamaica being punished. Some are working a treadmill. One is being flogged. (A nineteenth-century print)

▼ Wilberforce had to resign from Parliament in 1825 because he was ill. But he went on working for the abolition of slavery until just before his death, in 1833

slavery and the slave trade, and then used this information to persuade bishops, clergymen, MPs, merchants and landowners that slavery should be abolished.

Wilberforce and Clarkson

William Wilberforce was the most famous member of the committee. He was an MP, the son of a wealthy merchant, and a friend of several government ministers. He made speeches against slavery in the House of Commons, and worked hard to persuade his friends in the Government that slavery was wrong. But he was often ill, and he was not strong enough to travel long distances to interview sailors, traders and former slaves to get the information he needed. This work was done by Thomas Clarkson, who had won a prize for a Latin essay opposing slavery.

Clarkson put forward powerful arguments against slavery. He said that black people were not inferior to whites. He wrote:

'If the minds of Africans were unbroken by slavery, if they had the same expectations in life as other people, and the same opportunities ... they would be equal to the Europeans, and the argument that states them to be an inferior link in the chain of nature and designed for servitude ... is wholly false.'

Clarkson also argued that the slave trade was not necessary for the West Indies. He said that there were so many slaves there already there was no need to import any more. He even claimed that the planters would be better off if they freed all their slaves. He said that slaves worked slowly and unwillingly. Free men would work harder, and he pointed out that one planter, who had sold his slaves and employed free men instead, found that ten free men did the work of thirty slaves.

Clarkson travelled to Bristol and Liverpool to collect evidence. He interviewed sailors who had worked on slave ships. They told him that traders sometimes raided African villages and 'seized men, women and children as they found them in the huts', tied them up, and stowed them on board to sell in the West Indies. They gave details of how cruelly the slaves were treated on board ship, and also told Clarkson that many captains bullied and beat their crews.

In Bristol, Clarkson met a sailor who was dying as a result of being repeatedly knocked down by the captain of the *Alfred*. Another sailor had been flogged, and his arm had been broken. A third member of the ship's crew had been killed by being struck several times on the chest with a thick knotted rope. Clarkson went to the Deputy Town Clerk of Bristol, and asked him to arrest the *Alfred*'s captain. The clerk said there was no point, because the captain would either threaten or bribe the witnesses. He went on to tell Clarkson that he knew only one ship's captain in the slave trade who did not deserve to be hanged.

In Liverpool, Clarkson found more evidence. He saw slave irons, thumbscrews and mouth-openers on sale in the shops. When the Liverpool merchants heard he was there, they went to the inn where he was staying, argued with him, drank to 'the success of the trade', and insulted him. One evening nine men attacked him, and tried to push him off the pier. Clarkson was not discouraged. He had enough evidence to show how cruel the slave trade was, and he was able to prove that the death-rate among crews of slave ships was twenty times higher than on other ships sailing across the Atlantic. So instead of providing recruits for the Navy, the slave trade was killing them off.

The trade declines

The sugar-planters and their friends hated Wilberforce and Clarkson. Earl St Vincent, who

▼ These thumbscrews were collected by Clarkson on his travels. Try to work out how they were used

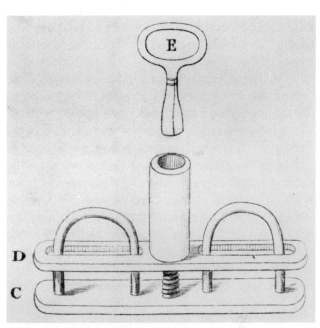

▲ Clarkson addresses an anti-slavery meeting. (A picture in a nineteenth-century magazine)

owned a plantation in the West Indies, said that Abolition was 'a damned and cursed doctrine held only by hypocrites'. Lord Nelson, whose wife came from the West Indies, agreed, speaking of the 'damnable doctrine of Wilberforce and his hypocritical allies'.

At first the planters were powerful enough to defeat the Abolitionists, but by the beginning of the nineteenth century, the slave trade with the West Indies was less important than it had been. Before 1783 many British merchant ships used to call in at American and West Indian ports on the same voyage. Some British ships stopped trading with America when the colonies became independent. This meant that the West Indies lost trade as well, because it was not worth crossing the Atlantic just to trade with the sugar-planters.

To make matters worse, Cuba and Brazil began to develop large, efficient plantations. They produced cheaper sugar than the West Indies. So the West Indian planters found it difficult to sell their sugar. Many reduced their output. Some closed down altogether. The demand for slaves fell, and the planters no longer needed to buy them from the traders.

▼ Numbers of slaves on Barbados, 1767–72. From 1767 to 1771, 24,172 slaves were imported into Barbados, but in 1772 there were only 60 more slaves there than in 1767

Year	Total no.	No. imported
1767	74,656	4,154
1768	76,275	4,628
1769	75,658	6,837
1770	76,334	5,825
1771	75,998	2,728
1772	74,716	—

Study 8

Use your imagination

1 Thomas Clarkson has been speaking at a meeting of an anti-slave trade committee, and has been asked these questions:

> What evidence have you to show that slaves are treated cruelly?
>
> How did you collect your evidence?

Write the answers that he might have given. (Think of a time when someone has doubted a statement that you know is true.)

2 An anti-slave trade committee has asked its members to write to their local newspaper, saying why they think that slavery should be banned in the British Empire. Write the letter that one member might have written. Remember to give the member's address and to sign the letter.
Mention:

> the reason why an anti-slave trade committee has been formed,
>
> an example to show that the trade is a cruel one,
>
> an example to show that free men work better than slaves.

(Think of something that you think should be abolished.)

3 Hugo Darcy has just returned from the West Indies. He believes that there are good reasons for supporting slavery. Write a letter that he might have sent to the newspaper *The Times*.
Mention:

> the reason why he thinks that slaves are better off in the West Indies than they would be in Africa,
>
> his opinion that slaves are better off than many British workers and that the public are told only about slaves who are badly treated,
>
> the fact that planters no longer need to import large numbers of slaves and the reasons why.

(Think of a movement today that is trying to abolish something that you support.)

Banning the slave trade

In 1807 Wilberforce and his friends brought a Bill into Parliament banning the slave trade. Planters found it difficult to argue that the trade was necessary. Several ministers favoured the Bill, and it was passed. It was now illegal for British ships to take part in the slave trade, and the Navy patrolled the coast of West Africa looking for vessels trying to break the new law. They stopped and searched British ships, but they had no right to stop foreign ships. So these continued to carry slaves across the Atlantic to the United States and Brazil.

The British did their best to persuade other countries to ban the slave trade, and in 1815 most European countries did so. In 1817 Spain and Portugal gave the British Navy the right to search their ships, but the trade still went on because Brazil and the United States continued to import slaves. Conditions on the voyage were even worse than before, because only rogues and villains stayed in the trade now that it was illegal, and they treated the slaves very cruelly.

The fight to abolish slavery

Although it was illegal to ship slaves across the Atlantic after 1807, it was still legal to own them in the West Indies. Wilberforce and his supporters now worked to persuade Parliament to abolish slavery itself.

First they concentrated on making sure that slaves were better treated. In 1823 the House of Commons ordered that in future all slaves should receive religious instruction, and said that they should be encouraged to marry and have families. Planters were forbidden to flog female slaves, and were only allowed to flog male slaves as a formal punishment—not just to make them work harder.

In spite of the regulations, many planters still treated slaves very harshly. James Stephen, an official in the Colonial Office, discovered that in 1829 in British Guiana over 20,000 official floggings were administered, amounting in all to two million lashes. In 1821 there had been 110,000 slaves in the colony. By 1832 there were fewer than 60,000. The rest had been worked to death.

In 1831 the slaves in Jamaica went on strike. Some set fire to the canefields, and four white people were murdered. In revenge the planters shot about a hundred slaves, and hanged 300. They blamed a Baptist missionary named Knibb for causing the strike, and made him leave the island.

The Abolitionists realised that it was impossible to persuade the planters to treat the slaves humanely. So they decided to campaign for the immediate abolition of slavery. At a general election in 1831, all the candidates were asked what they thought about slavery. To catch the imagination of the voters, posters were put up showing a planter flogging a young female slave, and black people in chains were paraded at public meetings.

The abolition of slavery, 1833

The majority of MPs elected in 1831 were opposed to slavery. Some believed it to be evil. Others thought it was out of date. They pointed out that British manufacturers, who were the most efficient in the world, paid labourers to work in their factories. They felt sure that the system of paying free labourers a wage would also work well on the plantations. So in 1833 Parliament passed an Act making it illegal to own slaves in all British colonies. The planters were paid £20 million in compensation—about £38 per slave.

Some West Indian planters were paid a great deal of money. The Earl of Crawford received £12,300, while John Gladstone was paid £85,600 for his slaves in British Guiana. Most slaves continued to work for their former owners for a small daily wage. Often they were not much better off than before. When the planters needed more labourers they sent agents to India, offering poor people a free passage to the West Indies if they would work on the plantations. Many Indians accepted this offer, so the planters still had enough workers.

Study 9

The struggle against slavery

1 (a) Copy the notes below:

   1807   Sl tr abolished in Br Emp.
           Br Navy couldn't stop foreign ships
           sl trading.

   (b) Complete your notes by saying briefly why
   each of these years was important in the
   struggle against slavery:

   1815   1817   1833

2 Most slave owners would not teach their slaves
   about Christianity because they did not want
   them to think that they were as good as their
   masters. Write brief notes saying what happened
   in

   (a) 1823, to make plantation owners teach their
   slaves about Christianity,
   (b) 1831, to make the plantation owners distrust
   the Christian missionaries.

3 Write brief notes under the heading 'The
   abolition of slavery, 1833', giving
   (a) one reason why slave owners were paid a
   great deal of money,
   (b) two reasons why planters still had enough
   low-paid workers to work the plantations.

The West Indies after 1833

The great days of the British West Indian sugar trade were over. It was cheaper to produce sugar on the huge plantations of Cuba and Brazil. At first the British Government taxed this 'foreign' sugar when it entered Britain to make it more expensive, and to encourage people to buy West Indian sugar. But in 1846 Sir Robert Peel, the Prime Minister, decided that people in Britain ought to be able to buy sugar at its proper price. So he lowered the duty year by year until in 1852 Cuban and Brazilian sugar was allowed in duty-free.

In British Guiana, Trinidad and Barbados, where plantations were large, the growers had enough money to buy new, efficient machinery and modernise their factories. But in Jamaica the plantations were smaller and growers had no money to spare. Many gave up growing sugar, and cultivated coffee or fruit, such as bananas.

But there was never enough work for the growing population of the West Indies. Many went to the United States to look for work, but in 1952 the Government of the United States stopped West Indians settling there. In the 1950s and 60s, the British Government encouraged West Indians to come and work in Britain's cities.

Study 10

The end of the sugar trade

Drawing

1 (a) Draw a poster that might have appeared in Britain in 1846, urging the Government to remove the duty on Cuban and Brazilian sugar.
  (b) Explain why Robert Peel thought the duty should be removed.

2 (a) Draw a poster urging the Government to help the West Indies by keeping the duty on Cuban and Brazilian sugar.
  (b) Explain why Jamaican planters could not compete with the plantations of Cuba and Brazil.

3 In the 1950s, the British Government was trying to set up a Welfare State in Britain, in which young people would be given a good education and anyone who was ill or needed help would be cared for. There were not enough workers in Britain to do all the jobs that had to be done, so advertisements were displayed in the West Indies, asking people to come to Britain to work.
  (a) Draw a poster that might have appeared in the West Indies in the 1950s, encouraging people to work in Britain.
  (b) Why were many West Indians unable to find work at home or in the U.S.A. after 1952?

Further work

Writing

1 (a) Find three or more examples to illustrate the statement, 'Slavery and sugar helped to make Britain prosperous in the eighteenth century.'
  (b) Turn this information into one or two paragraphs.

2 (a) Write brief notes to explain why each of these races of people settled in the West Indies:
    Europeans from Britain,
    Africans,
    Asians from India.
  (b) Turn your notes into an essay on 'The People of the West Indies, 1600 – 1900'.

3 (a) Write notes under these headings:
    'The growth of the West Indian sugar industry',
    'A plantation owner's life',
    'The great days come to an end'.
  (b) Turn your notes into an essay on 'Sugar and the West Indies, 1685 – 1852'.

Drawing and discussion

In groups of four:

1 Prepare a display that might have been used to win new supporters for an anti-slave trade committee.
  You should include:
    pictures to make people feel ashamed to allow slavery in the British Empire,

facts and figures to show that you know what you are talking about.
  Mount your displays in your classroom.

2 Decide which display you think would win most supporters for the committee, and be ready to give reasons why you have chosen it.

3 Ask someone to say which display he or she has chosen. Do the rest of you agree?

Figure it out

In 1772, Lord Chief Justice Mansfield declared that English law did not allow people to be slaves. After this judgment, many slaves in Britain were considered to be free. They took their masters' surnames and some of them married British workers.

At that time
    the white population of Britain was *c.* (about) 8,000,000,
    the black population of Britain was *c.* (about) 15,000.

1 In 1772, what was the ratio of black people to white in Britain?
    About 1 in 5,400,
    about 1 in 540,
    about 1 in 54.

2 Why may many people living in Britain today be descended from slaves who married British workers, but not know it?

3 The French Wars
1793 – 1815

A day in the life of Rifleman Harris

From Dorset to Portugal

John Harris was a soldier, and in 1808 he was in Portugal to fight the French. It was 20 August, and he was marching along a road near the town of Vimiero.

▲ An officer of the Rifle Regiment in full dress uniform. It looked very impressive, but made it difficult for him to move about on the battlefield

Harris came from Dorset. In 1803 he had been conscripted into the Army Reserve to defend Britain if the French invaded. In 1805 he was sent to Ireland, where he saw a group of soldiers in smart green uniforms. They were riflemen, and Harris thought they looked 'reckless and Devil-may-care'. So he decided to leave the Reserve and join the Rifle Regiment, even though it meant that he might be sent abroad. And now he was in Portugal.

Harris on the march

Harris was hot and tired. He was carrying a full kitbag, a greatcoat, a blanket, a camp kettle, a haversack full of shoe leather, a hammer, enough beef and biscuits for three days, a bottle full of water, a hatchet, a rifle and eighty rounds of ammunition. To make matters worse, he carried his load piled up behind his neck which forced his head forward and gave him a stiff neck.

Sentry duty

At last the day's march ended. Most of the men lay down to sleep, but Harris was posted to act as sentry. As he stood peering into the dark he heard footsteps approaching. He shouted, 'Who goes there?' There was no answer, so he raised his rifle and told the intruder to come forward slowly. Out of the darkness stepped an English officer— Major Napier. He looked hard at Harris and said, 'Be alert here, sentry, for I expect the enemy upon us tonight, and I know not how soon.'

Harris was frightened, and he was glad when another sentry came to relieve him and he could go and get a few hours' sleep in the safety of the camp.

Shoe repairs

Next morning Harris had to get up early. In civilian life he had been a cobbler, and in the Army he was expected to repair the shoes of the whole Regiment. So he was not surprised when a

▼ The Battle of Vimiero—an engraving made in 1817 for a book on Wellington's campaigns. Engravings like this were very popular, but they gave no idea of what a battle was really like

sergeant dug him in the ribs at sunrise and told him to get to work repairing a heap of boots and shoes.

Harris took his bag of leather and his tools, and made his way to a small stone hut halfway up a nearby hill. He sat down in the hut, picked up a boot and began to sew. Suddenly there was a crash, and part of the wall fell in, covering him with dust. A French cannonball had hit the building. The enemy had arrived.

The battle begins

Harris seized his rifle and hurried out, leaving the boots and shoes scattered on the floor. He joined his section, and they were ordered to go and occupy a windmill a short distance away.

They all set off at a run, but an officer called Harris back. He said, 'Harris, I shall not send you to that post. The cannon will play upon the mill in a few moments like hail—and what shall we do without our head shoe-maker to repair our shoes?'

So Harris stayed behind and watched a column of French soldiers advancing towards them. As it approached, the British cannon opened fire, and Harris saw 'regular lanes' torn through the French ranks by the cannonballs. Then Harris and the other riflemen scattered, lay down behind bushes or rocks and began to fire at the column.

In the thick of battle

Soon Harris was so busy loading and firing his rifle that he had no time to watch what anyone else was doing. In any case, for most of the time smoke from the rifles surrounded him like a fog, and he could see very little. He said afterwards:

'Very often I was obliged to stop firing, and dash [the smoke] aside from my face, and try in vain to get a sight of what was going on, whilst groans and shouts and a noise of cannon and musketry appeared almost to shake the very ground. It seemed Hell upon earth, I thought.'

When the French came close, the riflemen's bugler blew a call meaning 'fire and retire'. Then the riflemen fired a parting shot and withdrew. When the French retreated, the riflemen advanced again, lay down and waited for the next attack.

In one of these lulls Harris heard someone remark, 'Here comes Sir Arthur and his staff.' He turned round and saw the commander, Sir Arthur Wellesley, on horseback, greeting two other generals. It was Harris's only glimpse of Sir Arthur, who later became Duke of Wellington. Years later Harris said, 'It is something to have seen that wonderful man do even so common-place a thing as lift his hat to another on the battlefield.'

The final charge

Meanwhile the French were preparing another attack. They advanced, and the riflemen fired and retreated. The troops behind them could see that the French were hesitating, and the British general, Fane, drew his sword and ordered his men to charge. Many years later Harris described what happened next:

'Down came the whole line through a tremendous fire of cannon and musketry— and dreadful was the slaughter as they rushed onwards. As they came up with us, we sprang to our feet, gave one hearty cheer, and charged along with them, treading over our own dead and wounded who lay in the front ... The enemy turned and fled, the cavalry dashing upon them as they went off.'

Harris tripped and fell as he charged. He was tired, so he lay where he was for a short time, watching the cavalry officer who was leading the charge. 'With his sword waving in the air, he cheered the men on as he went dashing upon the enemy, and hewing and slashing at them in tremendous style.' Suddenly the officer fell. He had been shot dead.

After the battle

Harris pulled himself to his feet, and picked his way among the dead and wounded. An injured French soldier begged him for water. Harris gave him some and moved on, wandering among the dead to see if there was anything worth picking up. He found a British officer whose body had already been robbed, but whose shoes looked in quite good condition. So Harris sat down and tried them on. As he did, a shot rang out and a bullet whistled past his head. He turned, and was just in time to see a French soldier taking cover behind a small mound. So he seized his rifle and shot the Frenchman dead. 'I took it quite in the

▲ After a battle, rough carts pulled by bullocks took the wounded away. The carts had no springs, and the roads were rough

way of business,' he said. 'He had attempted my life and lost his own.'

Harris went up to the man he had shot and began to search the body. An officer came up. He said, 'What! Looking for money my lad, eh?' 'I am, sir,' answered Harris, 'but I cannot discover where this fellow has hidden his hoard.'

The officer said, 'You knocked him over in good style, and deserve something for the shot.' He pointed to the lining of the Frenchman's coat. 'Here is the place where they generally carry their coin.'

Harris thanked the officer, tore open the lining of the soldier's jacket and discovered a purse containing several silver coins. He pocketed the purse and returned to his company. Almost at once he was sent out on sentry duty. On his way he saw some biscuits spilling out of a dead man's haversack. He picked them up, scraped off the blood which spotted them, and ate them ravenously. It had been a long day, and he was hungry.

Harris fought in two more campaigns after Vimiero. But in 1809 he nearly died of fever, and was sent home. As soon as he was well enough, he opened a shoe-mender's shop in London, where he entertained his customers with stories of his life as a soldier.

Study 1

How do we know?

The Recollections of Rifleman Harris
The Recollections of Rifleman Harris is the name of a book that was published in 1829. 'Recollections' is another word for 'memories', and in the book Harris tells us what he remembers about his war service with the Rifle Regiment. Sometimes he wanders from the main point of his story because something he has just said reminds him of someone or something else he wants us to know about. He forgets some details that a historian would think were important, for example, the name of a town where his regiment was billeted. From what he tells us it is hard to understand *why* the British Army was in Portugal and *how* Wellington defeated the French at Vimiero.

Harris's recollections were written down by an army officer called Henry Curling, who probably took his shoes to be repaired at the shop Harris opened in London after the war. Curling liked talking to Harris and thought that other people would be interested in his stories.

1 Give an example of a detail that a historian would think was important but which Harris had forgotten.
2 Read the section of the story headed 'After the battle' on page 52. Why might you have expected Harris to remember his meeting with the French soldier?
3 Harris tells us when he cannot remember an important detail. Does this make you more or less willing to believe the information he claims he does remember? Give reasons for your answer.

What do you think?
Would *The Recollections of Rifleman Harris* be of any use to a historian who was writing a history of the Wars with France? Give reasons for your answer.

The Years of the Sword
In 1969 a writer called Elizabeth Longford published a biography of Sir Arthur Wellesley, called *Wellington: The Years of the Sword*. She wanted to show that Wellesley, who later became the Duke of Wellington, was a great general. She describes how Wellesley drew up his troops before the Battle of Vimiero began, why he gave certain orders when the fighting was going on, and how the French were defeated. This is how she describes one part of the battle:

'... in front of the village [of Vimiero] rose a green hump with a flat top, known ... as Vimiero Hill. ... Wellesley ... posted a strong skirmish line ... at the foot of Vimiero Hill, armed with rifles. Most of his infantry* waited behind the crest, with orders to hold their fire till the last moment ... As the French went in they were met in rapid succession by ... rifle-fire, a brief cannonade** and then, suddenly, a thin red line of British infantry ...'

* Foot-soldiers. British infantry wore red uniforms and were armed with muskets.
** A burst of cannon-fire.

At the end of her book, Elizabeth Longford gives a list of over 300 books, including *The Recollections of Rifleman Harris*, which gave her the information she needed to write *The Years of the Sword*.

1 The Battle of Vimiero was fought in 1808. How many years later was *The Years of the Sword* published?

2 Consider why Elizabeth Longford wrote her book. Why did she need to give a clear description of Vimiero?

3 Quote a sentence from Elizabeth Longford's description of the Battle of Vimiero that shows British riflemen took part in it.

What do you think?

Is it possible for a historian living today to have a clearer idea of what happened at the Battle of Vimiero than Rifleman Harris? Give reasons for your answer.

Understanding what happened

Harris at the Battle of Vimiero, 1808

Date	Time of Day	Events
20 Aug 1808	Evening	Br Army reaches Vimiero.
	Night	_____ _____
21 Aug 1808	Morning	The Fr attack. _____
	Afternoon	The Br drive off second Fr attack.
	Evening	_____ H is sent on sentry duty.

1 (a) Copy the timetable above, and use these notes to fill in the gaps correctly in the column headed 'Events':
   H sleeps but is wakened to mend shoes.
   H loots dead bodies.
   H goes on sentry duty.
   H goes into action against the Fr.
  (b) In which country did the Battle of Vimiero take place?

2 (a) Give an example to show how important it was for the riflemen to have good shoes.
  (b) Give an example to show that Harris
    (i) could be kind to his enemies,
    (ii) could kill without feeling guilty,
    (iii) looted bodies on the battlefield.

3 Wellesley's army was made up of riflemen and other infantrymen, artillerymen who fired the cannon, and cavalrymen who fought on horseback.
  (a) Read the sections headed 'The battle begins' and 'In the thick of battle', on pages 51 to 52. Were the riflemen expected
    (i) to drive back the advancing French troops,
    (ii) to break up the French advance so that the infantry and cavalry could drive them back?
  (b) Why was a rifleman
    (i) often unable to see much when he was fighting,
    (ii) able to hear his orders?

Further work

Writing

1 After the War, Harris might have told a customer who came to his shop, 'I was mending shoes when the Battle of Vimiero began.' Write what he might have gone on to say about the morning of the battle, from the time the sergeant woke him up to his first sight of the advancing French column.

2 Twenty years after the Battle of Vimiero, a Frenchman remembers how Harris gave him a drink of water. He tells his friends about the English rifleman who was kind to him and says what has just reminded him of the incident. Write what he might have said.

3 (a) Make a list of three or more notes under each of these headings:

> Uniform and kit in the Rifle Regiment,
> Advantages and disadvantages of being the Regiment's shoe-mender,
> After the Battle of Vimiero.

(b) Under the heading 'Fighting in the Rifle Regiment', write two or three sentences saying why a man might have liked the idea of joining the Regiment.

(c) Complete your essay by turning your notes into three paragraphs.

Drawing

1 In a song written in the eighteenth century, a young woman asks the soldier who is leaving her:

> 'Why must you go away, fighting for strangers,
> When you could stay at home, free from all dangers?'

(a) Draw a picture to illustrate the song.

(b) What made Harris decide to volunteer for the Rifle Regiment?

2 (a) Draw a book cover for
   (i) *The Recollections of Rifleman Harris*,
   (ii) *Wellington: The Years of the Sword*.

(b) Why would someone studying the Battle of Vimiero need to read both books?

3 Draw a picture to illustrate one or more of the following quotations from the story of Rifleman Harris:

> 'Be alert here, sentry ...'
> 'It seemed Hell upon earth.'
> 'He had attempted my life and lost his own.'

Drama

The engravings of the Battle of Vimiero give no idea of the noise of the battle.

In groups of four:

1 Divide the story of Rifleman Harris into as many sections as you have groups, and give each group a section to prepare.

2 Choose some people in your group to be readers and some to produce sound effects. Rehearse your reading.

3 Perform your readings as a class.

Glossary

Add the words below to your glossary and explain, in your own words, what each of them means:

> infantry   civilian

The Revolutionary Wars

Rifleman Harris was one of thousands of British soldiers and sailors who fought in wars against the French between 1793 and 1815. War broke out as a result of the French Revolution, which began in 1789. The revolutionaries declared that all men are equal, abolished the Church, and executed the king and many of the rich landowners. Then they tried to start revolutions in other countries. This upset the rulers of most of the rest of Europe, and soon France was at war with Austria and Holland. The French armies were very successful, and by the beginning of 1793 they controlled the whole of the Low Countries, including the ports along the River Scheldt.

This brought Britain into the War. A hundred years earlier the British had fought a long war to keep the French out of the Low Countries. Since 1713 the Dutch coast and the River Scheldt had been controlled by Britain's ally, Holland, whose Government prevented other countries from trading there. Now the French were in charge, and to make matters worse they opened the Scheldt ports to the ships of all nations.

British merchants feared that fewer ships would come to London, and thought the French might use the Dutch ports as bases to attack

▼ A Frenchman wearing a revolutionary cap. The ribbons of the rosette are red, white and blue—the same colours as the Tricolour, the flag of the Revolution

Britain's ships. So in September 1793 the British went to war against the French, determined to drive them out of the Low Countries.

Table 1: The War against France

1789	The French Revolution begins when a mob destroys the Bastille, the French state prison in Paris.
1792	France becomes a republic. The French declare the River Scheldt open to the ships of all countries.
1793	The French king, Louis XVI, is executed. War breaks out.
1796	Napoleon, a French republican general, conquers Italy.
1797	The British Navy defeats the Dutch fleet at Camperdown in the North Sea, and the Spanish at Cape St Vincent in the Atlantic.
1798	Napoleon invades Egypt. Nelson traps his army there by sinking the French fleet at the Battle of the Nile.
1801	The Danes try to close the Baltic to British ships. Nelson sinks the Danish fleet at Copenhagen to keep the Baltic open for trade with Britain.
1804	Napoleon becomes Emperor of France.
1805	The Battle of Trafalgar finally gives Britain control of the seas.

Study 2

The French Revolution and Europe

Britain controls the River Scheldt, 1713 – 1793

Date	Event
1713	Br gains control of the trade along the R Scheldt.
_____	Revolution in Fr.
_____	Fr invades Holland and opens R Scheldt to trading ships of all nations.
_____	

1 (a) Draw the picture of the revolutionary cap on page 56.

(b) List three things that the revolutionaries believed in or did that led to war with Austria and Holland.

2 (a) Copy the time-chart above.

(b) Complete your chart by adding (i) the missing dates, (ii) the notes below, in the correct places:

Br declares war on Fr.

Holland, Br ally, guards the Dutch coast & R Scheldt.

Fr tries to spread the Revolution.

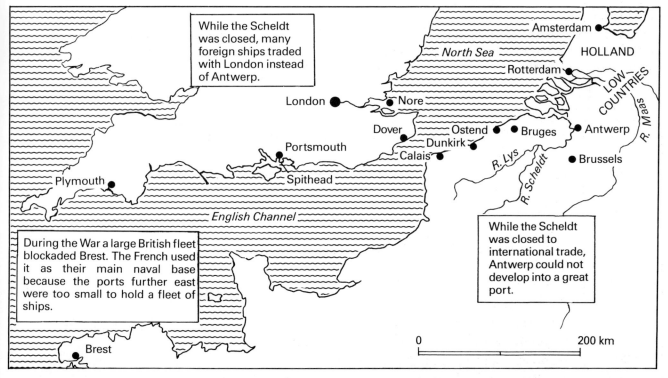

While the Scheldt was closed, many foreign ships traded with London instead of Antwerp.

During the War a large British fleet blockaded Brest. The French used it as their main naval base because the ports further east were too small to hold a fleet of ships.

While the Scheldt was closed to international trade, Antwerp could not develop into a great port.

3 (a) Copy the sketch-map above.

(b) Using the information in the map explain why

(i) London merchants wanted the Scheldt to remain closed,

(ii) the French would have found the Dutch ports useful if they went to war with Britain.

The War at sea

The Channel fleet

In the early years of the War, most of the fighting between the British and the French took place at sea. The British Navy had a strong force of ships at each end of the English Channel to defend the south coast against invasion.

The best ships were sent to patrol the western end of the Channel, to make sure that the French fleet did not leave its base at Brest. The Channel fleet was kept at sea for many months at a time, sailing to and fro off the French coast. When provisions ran short, transport ships sailed out with fresh meat, vegetables, beer and water. A warship was only allowed to leave for home if it needed major repairs. The Channel fleet had a difficult and dangerous job. To guard the coast properly, ships had to stay close to the shore, and if a gale sprang up they were likely to be wrecked.

Keeping the ships at sea

It was difficult to keep a large fleet at sea in the eighteenth century. The ships were made of wood. They had oak hulls, elm keels and pine masts. It took an enormous amount of wood to build a warship. Eleven elms and more than 2,000 oaks had to be felled to make the British flagship HMS *Victory*. By the middle of the eighteenth century, Britain was running short of good timber. This meant that some ships were built from unseasoned wood—which shrank and rotted when they were at sea. Many captains complained. Sir John Jervis said his ship was 'a complete sieve', while Captain Collingwood's ship was so rotten that only a strip of copper nailed to the hull stopped it sinking. Most French and Spanish ships were better designed and more strongly built than the British ships.

▲ HMS *Victory* took six years to build, and cost just over £63,000. It carried 104 guns, and was on active service from 1778 until 1812, usually as flagship of the fleet. It is now in dry dock in Portsmouth. This engraving was made in 1818

Manning a warship

A large sailing-ship was a very complicated machine, driven by the wind, and a man-of-war, or warship, needed a large crew of skilled men to work it. The sails were held in position by a huge number of ropes, some of which had to be adjusted whenever the wind changed or the ship altered course. In battle, ships had to move quickly. Sails had to be let out or taken in at a moment's notice. Some men had to clamber into the rigging, while on deck others hauled away at ropes, with cannon-shot and musket-balls whistling round them.

A warship's crew spent so long practising the drills they might have to use in battle that they could do them without thinking. One onlooker noticed that the first lieutenant of the *Unité* had only to say two words—'Make sail'—and in a few moments the bare masts of the ship were covered in sails. It was done so quickly he could hardly believe his eyes. Because they spent so many hours practising what they had to do, most British sailors worked better than those of other countries. Their courage and skill more than made up for the poor quality of some of the British ships.

Study 3

Guarding the Channel

1 You have learnt that ∵ is the abbreviation for *because*.

Now remember that ∴ is the abbreviation for *therefore*.

These abbreviations will help you to make your notes more quickly.

Copy the notes below, using the abbreviations for *because* and *therefore* instead of the words.

> The Br feared the Fr would invade S Brit, *therefore* they sent their best ships to blockade the Fr base at Brest.
>
> It was difficult to keep a large fleet at sea *because* the ships were made of unseasoned wood, *therefore* they rotted.
>
> Br crews were highly trained, *therefore* their skill made up for the poor quality of their ships.

2 (a) Read the section headed 'The War at sea' opposite.

(b) Complete the notes below, using the abbreviation for *therefore*.

> Br ships could not return to base for fresh provisions, ...
>
> Enormous numbers of Br trees were felled to make warships, ...
>
> In battle a warship's crew had to perform tasks quickly and calmly, ...

3 (a) Using the abbreviations ∵ and ∴ write a list of notes showing why a captain in the Navy had a hard job in wartime.

(b) Write a paragraph under the heading 'A difficult and dangerous job', turning your notes into sentences.

Manning the Navy

Naval officers

Naval officers usually came from middle- or upper-class families and joined up as midshipmen—the lowest rank of officer—often as young as twelve or thirteen years old. There were several midshipmen on every man-of-war, and they had to work hard. They climbed in the rigging to help set sails, kept watch, learnt how to work out the ship's position, and took command of the longboat whenever it left the ship. It was strange to see rough, experienced sailors rowing a boat commanded by a boy of thirteen.

At the age of twenty, every midshipman who had been in the Navy for six years or more was interviewed by a committee of three captains. If they decided he knew his job, he would be promoted to lieutenant, and eventually to

▲ This young midshipman is carrying a sextant, used to help fix the ship's position when at sea

Prize money

Rank	Amount to each (£)
Captain	65,000
Lieutenants	13,000
Warrant officers	4,300
Petty officers	1,800
Seamen	485

commander and captain.

Officers had reasonably good pay, and if they captured an enemy ship they were paid a good share of its value as prize money.

The table above shows how the money due to HMS *Active* was divided up. The ship was captured in 1762, and its cargo was valued at £520,000. The admiral in charge of the fleet received £64,000, even though he had played no part in the capture.

In wartime the officers spent most of their time at sea. In peacetime many ships were laid up, and their officers were sent ashore on half pay.

Ordinary seamen

Ordinary seamen were treated quite differently from the officers. Seamen were taken on for as long as they were needed. They were paid nineteen shillings a month, plus a small share in any prize money due to a ship. Their pay in 1796 was the same as it had been in 1660, though since then prices had risen by about fifty per cent. The men were rarely paid on time. They were often owed nearly a year's pay. To make matters worse, the authorities deducted money from their pay to spend on the hospital for retired sailors at Greenwich, or to make up the salaries of ships' chaplains. Sailors on merchant ships were much better off. They could earn up to £5 a month, and if they did not like their ship they could leave it at the end of the voyage.

Food and fitness

Sailors in the Navy were usually badly fed. In port they had fresh meat and vegetables, but by the time they had been at sea for a few weeks there were none left. Then they had to eat salt meat, biscuits which a thirteen-year-old midshipman described as 'very good indeed, but rather maggoty', and cheese which, according to one journalist, was so hard that sailors sometimes used it to make buttons. They had beer to drink, but it was often sour. They also had grog—a mixture of one part dark rum to three parts stinking water—and a small quantity of sweetened lemon juice.

Some dealers who supplied the Navy were dishonest. They sent flour and meat which had been lying in their stores for months, and were already half rotten. They also used false weights and measures, and supplied less than they were paid for. Captains complained, but nothing was done about it because the dealers bribed the officials who were in charge of supplying the ships.

It was difficult to keep fit on such a poor diet, but sailors were healthier at the end of the eighteenth century than they had been in the past. The lemon juice protected them against scurvy, and many ships had ventilating systems circulating fresh air to the crew's quarters down below. Ships were kept clean and tidy. Crews spent much time scrubbing the decks.

Jumping to it

Discipline in the Navy was very strict. In battle the safety of the ship depended on everybody doing exactly as he was told, at once. Sailors were therefore taught to 'jump to it', and on many ships those who hesitated when given an order got a blow from a rope's end. More serious crimes were punished by flogging with a cat-o'-nine-tails—a whip with nine cords. Some captains believed it was impossible to keep order without flogging. Others refused to allow any corporal punishment. They believed that if men were well treated they would work harder. These captains usually had happy, well-run ships, just as efficient as those on which sailors were beaten.

Recruiting and the Press Gangs

In wartime the Navy needed more than 100,000 sailors. Stories of poor pay, bad food and harsh treatment made it difficult to get enough recruits. The Admiralty encouraged men to volunteer by offering them a bonus of £5 each when they signed on. Then in 1795 Parliament passed an Act

▲ This engraving by George Cruikshank (1792–1878) shows a flogging. A captain could sentence any of his crew to twelve lashes from the 'cat'. A court martial could order up to 300 lashes, which sometimes killed the victim

▼ Sailors lived beside their guns. The tables at which they ate were slung from the ceiling and could be stowed away when space was needed to work the

guns. (One of a series of engravings, called *The Sailor's Progress*, drawn by George Cruikshank in 1819)

ordering each county to provide a certain number of men for the Navy. There were still not enough, so the Government was forced to use Press Gangs—bands of armed sailors commanded by a lieutenant. These gangs roamed the streets of ports and boarded merchant ships, in search of experienced sailors between eighteen and fifty-five years of age. They seized those they found, dragged them on board ship and enrolled them as members of the crew. Sometimes a Press Gang would catch very few men. Occasionally, if a merchant ship had just docked, they might bring in more than 100 in a night.

Nobody liked Press Gangs, but without them the Navy would not have had enough men. In 1800 half the seamen in the king's ships had been forced to join by Press Gangs. As a rule sailors put up with low pay and bad food. But in 1797, when the War with France was at its height and Britain was in danger of being invaded, the crews of the fleets at Spithead and the Nore mutinied and refused to put to sea until they had been promised more pay and better food. The Admiralty gave way. A seaman's pay was raised by three shillings a month, and dealers were ordered to supply the correct amount of good fresh food.

Study 4

Should Richard Parker die?

Richard Parker was the leader of the mutineers at the Nore. The crews of some ships there refused to join the mutiny, and Parker ordered his men to open fire on them. When the mutiny was over, Parker was hanged. Later a medical student made this cast of his face.

1 Read the section headed 'Manning the Navy' on pages 60 to 62.
2 Divide into two groups, one to defend and one to prosecute Parker.
3 (a) Consider:
    pay and conditions in the Navy,
    the danger of a French invasion,
    anything else you think is important.
  (b) According to whether you are defending or prosecuting Parker, make a list of three or more reasons *either* why his life should be spared, *or* why he should be put to death.
4 Choose one person from each side to put his or her case to the class. What do the rest of you think?
5 Take a vote to decide whether or not Parker's execution was justified.

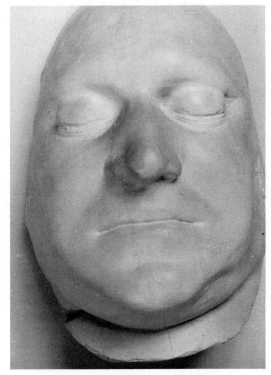

▲ The death-mask of Richard Parker

The British fleet in battle

The British fleet usually won its battles. This was partly because British crews were better trained, and partly because Admiral Howe had thought out new tactics to use in sea battles. As a rule, in the eighteenth century a fleet sailed into battle with its ships in a long line, one behind the other. As two enemy fleets came close to each other they fired their cannon. French and Spanish commanders liked to fight at a distance, aiming shots at the masts and rigging of their enemies. The British, on the other hand, liked to fight at close quarters, and fired into the hulls of the enemy fleet. They did not sink many ships. At close range, cannonballs passed straight through a wooden ship—in one side and out the other.

As long as both fleets kept in line the French usually managed to keep their distance, and the British ships did little damage. So Howe ordered his ships to sail straight at the enemy line from the side. This was so unexpected that enemy captains were not sure what to do. Some tried to sail straight on. Others stopped. Soon the line broke up, and the British ships closed in, firing broadsides into the enemy at point-blank range.

The Battle of Trafalgar

Admiral Nelson

Britain's best admiral was Lord Nelson. He defeated the French in several naval battles. In 1801, when Denmark, Sweden, Russia and Prussia banned British ships from trading in the Baltic, he attacked and sank the Danish fleet in Copenhagen Harbour. Denmark and her allies no longer had enough ships to keep the Baltic closed, and British merchants were able to continue trading there, buying the hemp and timber Britain needed for her ships.

The importance of Trafalgar

Nelson's last battle was off the Spanish coast near Cape Trafalgar in October 1805. It was the most important sea battle of the War, and was fought between a British fleet of twenty-seven ships and a combined French and Spanish fleet of thirty-three ships. If the British had lost, France and Spain would have been able to cut off Britain's trade. They might even have been able to invade Britain. So a great deal was at stake as the two fleets approached each other.

Preparations for the battle

The enemy fleet was drawn up in a line. The British fleet was in two columns, one led by Nelson in the *Victory*, and the other by his second-in-command, Collingwood, in the *Royal Sovereign*. Nelson planned to break through the enemy line in two places, and had ordered his captains to do 'whatever they thought best, provided it led them quickly and closely alongside an enemy'.

The wind was very light and the ships moved slowly, so there was plenty of time to prepare for battle. On every ship men cleared furniture from the cabins and stowed it in the hold. Cooks put out the fires in the galleys, the crew moved their belongings from the gun decks, opened the gunports, and ran out the guns. Boys brought powder up from the magazines, gunners loaded their cannon and lit the matches. Sand was thrown over the decks to prevent men slipping as they moved about, and most of the crew stripped to the waist. They knew it would be more difficult for surgeons to clean their wounds if a shot had passed through their clothes and carried bits of cloth into their bodies.

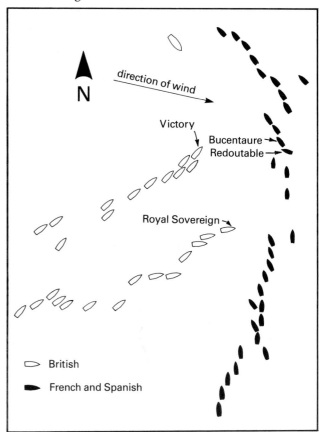

▼ This plan shows the two fleets just before the Battle of Trafalgar

Meanwhile, down below in the dark cockpit, the surgeons and their mates lit their lanterns and laid out saws and dressings. They were pleased it was calm. It was almost impossible to dress wounds and amputate limbs when the ship was rolling and pitching in a gale.

In another part of the ship, the carpenter was preparing wooden plugs to stop up the holes that enemy cannon-shot would make in the hull. When all the preparations were complete the men waited. Some sharpened cutlasses. Others polished the guns. A few danced a hornpipe. 'The hope of prize money makes them happy,' said an officer.

The fleets meet in battle

As the two fleets came closer, the French and Spanish ships began to fire. The British did not reply. They were determined not to fire until they were really close. The *Royal Sovereign*, whose hull had just been covered in new copper sheeting, slid through the water more quickly than the *Victory*, and was the first to get alongside a French ship, but a few minutes later Nelson's ship was also among the enemy. She fired a broadside at the *Bucentaure*, and then crashed into the *Redoutable*, a much smaller vessel. The two ships locked together. The *Victory* fired broadside after broadside. Her gun decks were filled with bitter-smelling smoke, while up on her main deck there were shouts and screams as shot from the French ship ripped at point-blank range into the bodies of men crouching behind the rails.

A cannonball shattered the wheel, and the *Victory* had to be steered by a tiller below decks. In spite of the danger Nelson remained on his quarter-deck—an easy target in his admiral's uniform. A French marksman perched in the *Redoutable*'s rigging took careful aim and fired. His bullet struck Nelson just under the left shoulder, passed through his chest, and shattered his spine. The wounded Admiral was carried down below, and within two hours he was dead.

Britain rules the waves

As Nelson lay dying, his fleet was winning a great victory. By nightfall, eighteen enemy ships had surrendered. Four more were captured later. Only eleven returned to Cadiz, and they never left port again. The British fleet had suffered too. Nearly 1,700 men had been killed or seriously wounded, and almost all the ships were damaged, with ragged sails and hulls full of shot-holes. But even this battered fleet was stronger than that of any other country. After Trafalgar, Britain ruled the waves until the end of the nineteenth century.

▲ Many romantic pictures were painted of the death of Nelson. His body was brought back to Britain in a cask of brandy, and was buried in St Paul's Cathedral. This engraving of a painting by Daniel Maclise (1806–1870) was made in 1876

Study 5

Fighting at Trafalgar, 1805

1 Read the section headed 'The Battle of Trafalgar' on pages 64 to 65.
   (a) Copy the plan of the Battle of Trafalgar on page 64.
   (b) Complete the notes opposite, using these abbreviations to fill in the gaps correctly. (You have used them all before, except ⚔ which stands for *battle*.)

   ⚔ Br ∴ Sp Fr

The Battle of Trafalgar, 1805

Fr & _____ were allies, _____ Br had to fight two fleets.
If the _____ & Sp won the _____ they could have
   taken control of the sea,
   cut off trade with _____ ,
   attempted to invade Br.
Admiral Nelson and the Br fleet won the _____ of Trafalgar, _____ Br ruled the waves.

---

2 Write notes explaining why, before a battle, sailors used to
   move their belongings,
   throw sand on the decks,
   strip to the waist.

3 Write notes explaining why
   Nelson wanted his captains to get as near to the enemy as possible,
   the *Victory* and the *Redoutable* could not get away from each other,
   Nelson was an easy target for the French marksman.

The War on land

Napoleon's army

While the British Navy was beating the French at sea, the French Army, commanded by their great general Napoleon, was defeating the armies of almost every country in Europe. Napoleon fought his battles in a new way. Instead of drawing his army up in long lines facing the enemy, he arranged them in columns. When the time came to charge, the columns dashed forward, shouting and waving their swords and muskets. They smashed through the lines of soldiers facing them, and then fanned out, stabbing and shooting their startled enemy, who had never been taught how to deal with such an attack.

By 1808 Napoleon and his armies seemed unbeatable. Many troops felt there was no point in fighting them, and ran away before a battle began. But two British generals, Sir John Moore and Sir Arthur Wellesley (who afterwards became Duke of Wellington) believed that the British Army could beat the French.

British tactics

Since their defeat in America, the British had improved their tactics. They armed some of their troops with rifles and trained them to use their common sense. Riflemen like Harris were allowed to choose their own positions in a battle, and fire when they thought best. The rest of the Army was taught exactly what to do in a battle. Moore and Wellington realised that a long line of troops ought to be able to stop a column that was charging towards them. Only a few troops in the column could fire at the line, but everybody in the line could fire at the column. So British troops were taught to stand and wait in silence while the column approached. Then, when the enemy were about 50 m away, the men in line fired, killing or wounding many of those at the front of the column and stopping its advance.

Wellington's campaigns

Wellington's new tactics worked. Moore was killed in battle in 1809, but Wellington fought several campaigns in Spain and Portugal between 1808 and 1813. He hardly ever made a mistake. He always made sure that his men were properly fed and equipped, though—unlike many generals—he did not insist that they always wore their full uniform. An officer in his army, Lieutenant Grattan, wrote: 'Provided we brought our men into the field with sixty rounds of good ammunition each, he never looked to see whether their trousers were black, blue or grey.' In battle he always seemed to be where he was needed, and he gave his orders quickly and clearly.

Wellington's career

British officers had to pay to join the Army. Anyone who had the money could buy a commission in a British regiment. Rich landowners put their sons in the Army if they could not think of any other career for them.

This was what happened to Wellington. He was a lazy boy. He was quiet, and seemed interested only in playing the violin. His mother, the Countess of Mornington, complained, 'I vow to God I don't know what I shall do with my awkward son Arthur.' Eventually she decided he was 'food for powder, nothing more', and put him in the Army.

So at the age of eighteen Wellington became an army officer. He decided to try to understand his profession. He burnt his violin, and read books about drill and battle-tactics. He borrowed

▲ On 2 May 1808, a rebellion broke out in Madrid, the capital of Spain, and some French troops were killed. The next day French soldiers rounded up civilians and shot them. This picture is by the Spanish artist, Goya (1746 – 1828)

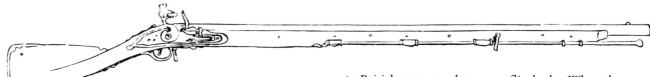

▲ British army muskets were flintlocks. When the trigger was pulled, the flint in the hammer struck a spark off the metal plate in front of it. This ignited a small quantity of gunpowder placed over a hole leading into the gun barrel, and so fired the powder behind the bullet

money to buy himself a higher rank, and by the time he was twenty-four he was a lieutenant colonel in command of 2,000 men.

Wellington's elder brother was sent to India as governor-general, and took Wellington with him. In 1802, just before his thirty-third birthday, Wellington was made a general, and a year later he commanded an army in battle for the first time. He said afterwards that one of the reasons he was so successful as a general was that he began commanding armies when he was young, and had plenty of time to learn his trade.

Wellington's officers

Some officers bought commissions in the Army and then could not afford to pay to be promoted. So a few fifty-year-old officers were still only lieutenants or captains. They felt very bitter when they saw all the highest ranks filled by rich young men, especially as some of them did not know much about the Army.

Many officers took their jobs seriously, but others were interested only in drinking, hunting and gambling. Some were too stupid or too unreliable to command men in battle. In 1810 Wellington was sent the names of three officers who were going to join his army in Portugal. 'The first,' he wrote to a friend in the War Office, 'I have generally understood to be a madman. I believe it is your opinion that the second is not very wise. The third will, I believe, be a useful man.' He then complained about some of his other officers. He called one general 'a disgrace to the Army', and wrote, 'When I consider that these are the persons on whom I am to rely to lead columns against the French generals, I tremble.'

To try to make sure that nothing went wrong, Wellington always gave the most important jobs to officers he could trust. Other officers were given posts where they could do no harm.

Wellington's troops

The soldiers in Wellington's army had all signed on for twenty-one years. When they joined they received a bounty of between £10 and £25 each, and by 1812 their pay was a shilling a day—twice what a soldier's pay had been forty years earlier.

Once, in a fit of temper, Wellington said that his army was 'the scum of the earth, enlisted for drink', and it is true that many of them were rough, hard-drinking men always on the look out for something to steal. They were at their worst just after a victory or when they were retreating. After their victory at the Battle of Vitoria in 1813, the troops spent the whole night plundering and drinking, and as a result were unable to pursue the enemy the next morning. In 1812 when they had to retreat from Burgos to Madrid, 12,000 soldiers got drunk. Many were captured by the enemy, while others, drunkenly hunting for pigs in a forest, shot two fellow soldiers dead by mistake.

If troops did not do as they were ordered they could be tried by court martial, and sentenced to be flogged. For serious offences they could be hanged or shot. Some officers believed that flogging was the only way to control troops. Colonel Craufurd sentenced a man to 300 lashes for criticising him behind his back. He insisted that the whole regiment was drawn up to watch the punishment, even though the French were about to attack them.

Other officers thought that men behaved better if they were well treated. So they got to know their troops, talked and listened to them patiently, and even called them by their first names. They found that it was hardly ever necessary to order a man to be flogged.

British soldiers were at their best in battle. They obeyed orders instantly, fought with great courage, and were always ready to attack. Many were Scottish Highlanders or Irishmen who joined the Army because they could not make a living in their own countries. They were good soldiers. They were used to poor food, wet clothing, damp houses, uncomfortable beds and a damp climate. In fact, in Wellington's army, they were in some ways better off than at home, for they were usually well fed, and had warm uniforms to wear.

Women in the War

Army regulations allowed six women to travel overseas with each company of troops. There were about a hundred men in a company. As a rule nobody bothered to make sure the regulations were obeyed, and many soldiers were accompanied by their wives.

The women had a hard life. Rifleman Harris remembered them following the troops on foot through Spain and Portugal. On long marches some carried their husbands' muskets or knapsacks, and Harris noticed that they had more stamina than the men. One winter's day he saw a pregnant woman sink down in the snow at the side of the road. He thought she was dying, but the next day he saw her again, walking along with a tiny baby in her arms.

When there was a battle the women had to stay behind the lines. If their husbands did not return at the end of the day, the women went to search for them among the dead and wounded. After the Battle of Rolica in 1808, Harris watched one woman who found her husband dead. She kissed him, knelt beside him, took a prayer book from her pocket and read the burial service over his body. She then rejoined the other women, and the next day travelled on with the Army. Harris became very attached to her, and asked her to marry him. She refused, saying that 'she had received too great a shock on the occasion of her husband's death ever to think of another soldier'. A few days later the Army reached Lisbon, where she found a ship to take her back to England.

▲ Soldiers and their wives on the march. (An engraving by the cartoonist Rowlandson)

Study 6

Wellington's army

1 (a) Draw a soldier's wife from the picture of soldiers on the march on page 69.
  (b) Copy the statement opposite that you think is correct.
  (c) List three or more examples to illustrate the statement that you have chosen.

Soldiers' wives had to look after themselves and their husbands.
Soldiers' wives were well looked-after by the British Army.

2 (a) Draw a picture of an army officer. (Use the picture on page 50 to help you.)
  (b) Copy the statement opposite that you think is correct.
  (c) List three or more examples to illustrate the statement that you have chosen.

Many good officers in the Army remained captains because they could not afford to buy a higher rank.
Officers in the Army were promoted if they showed that they were good leaders.

3 (a) Copy the statement opposite that you think is correct.
  (b) List three or more examples to illustrate the statement that you have chosen.
  (c) Draw a picture to illustrate your idea of 'Wellington in battle'.

Wellington was lazy, thought his troops were useless drunkards and was lucky to win any battles.
Wellington took his work seriously and was a strict disciplinarian, but he did not fuss about unimportant details.

The end of the Wars

Napoleon surrenders

In 1813 Wellington drove the French Army out of Spain, and in 1814 he invaded southern France. Meanwhile, in Germany, the armies of Russia, Austria and Prussia, defeated Napoleon at the Battle of Leipzig.

In April 1814 Napoleon surrendered, and was sent to live in exile on the Mediterranean island of Elba. The Wars seemed to be over. Wellington's army, which had fought so well in Spain and Portugal, was disbanded. Some of the troops returned to Britain and others were sent to America. 'I could have done anything with that army,' said Wellington many years later, 'it was in such perfect order.'

Napoleon returns

Napoleon did not stay long on Elba. In March 1815 he decided to return to France. He landed on the south coast and made his way to Paris, where he was proclaimed emperor. In June he invaded Belgium. Wellington was put in charge of an allied army of 70,000 men to defend Brussels. He drew up his army at Waterloo, just south of the city, and waited for Napoleon to attack.

Waterloo, 1815

By 1815 Wellington had defeated many of Napoleon's best generals. But he never fought against Napoleon himself until they met at Waterloo. It was a long hard battle. Napoleon first attacked Wellington's line with cavalry. Galloping horses could easily break through a line of soldiers, so as the cavalry approached, Wellington's troops left their lines and formed up in squares. Each side of the square consisted of three ranks of soldiers facing outwards. The men in the front rank knelt down with their muskets and bayonets pointing in front of them. The horses could not ride straight at the squares without spearing themselves on the bayonets. So instead they rode round the squares, and the soldiers in the second and third ranks fired at

Table 2: The War against France

1806	The Berlin Decrees. Napoleon bans all ships coming from Britain and her colonies from trading with any port under French control.
1807	By the Orders in Council Britain instructs all ships trading with France and her allies to call at a British port first to have their cargo checked, so that Britain can control which goods are shipped to France.
1807	By the Milan Decrees Napoleon orders all ships calling at British ports to be seized. French armies invade Spain and Portugal.
1808	A British army commanded by Sir Arthur Wellesley is sent to Portugal.
1812	Napoleon invades Russia and has to retreat, losing most of his army.
1813	Wellington defeats the French at the Battle of Vitoria, and drives them out of Spain.
1814	Napoleon surrenders, and is exiled to Elba.
1815	Napoleon returns to France, but is finally defeated at Waterloo.

them with the muskets. As soon as the cavalry rode off, the men went back into line.

When Napoleon saw that his cavalry could not drive the enemy from the field, he sent in columns of infantry. As usual, the lines of men drove them back. Afterwards Wellington wrote that the French Army 'just moved forward in the old style in columns, and was driven off in the old style'. By evening the French had lost thousands of men, and those who were left were tired and shaken. What was more, a Prussian army was on its way to help Wellington. Napoleon ordered his army to retreat, leaving Wellington victorious.

Wellington's army had suffered too. Those who were not injured had been fighting all day, half-blinded by smoke and deafened by gunfire.

Captain Mercer of the artillery said his men were 'worn out, their clothes, faces etc. blackened by the smoke and spattered all over with mud and blood'. Above all they were thirsty. Most of them had drunk nothing all day.

Dead and wounded were lying all over the field. Mercer saw injured men trying to bandage their wounds while others rose, staggered a few feet, and then collapsed again. The shouts and groans of wounded men mingled with the 'melancholy neighing' of dying horses. Mercer found one horse with both its back legs shot off. He wrote, 'Although I knew that killing him at once would be a mercy, I could not.' He had seen so much blood shed during the battle that he was 'sickened at the thought of shedding more'.

▲ One corner of a British 'square' under attack from enemy cavalry

Wellington felt much the same as Mercer. He said, 'I don't know what it is to lose a battle, but certainly nothing can be more painful than to gain one with the loss of so many of one's friends.' A few days later he remarked, 'I hope to God that I have fought my last battle. It is a bad thing to be always fighting.' Wellington got his wish. Waterloo was the last battle in the War between Britain and France which had begun in 1793.

The old soldiers

In his last order to the troops who had fought with him in Spain and Portugal, Wellington wrote that he 'would never cease to feel the warmest interest in their welfare and honour', and that he 'would be at all times happy to be of any service' to them.

He kept his word. For as long as he lived, he carried sovereigns in his pocket to give to old soldiers who approached him. He also helped them in other ways. One who had lost his job called at his country house to ask for help.

'Do you know anything of gardening?' asked Wellington.
'No, your Grace.'
'Then learn, *learn* and return this day fortnight at the same hour. Take the place of gardener at Walmer Castle.'
'But I know nothing of gardening.'
'Neither do I, neither do I,' said Wellington.

The old soldier, Sergeant Townsend, got the job of head gardener at Walmer Castle and kept it for many years.

▼ After Waterloo, prize money was distributed to the British soldiers

Rank	Amount to each (£)
Commander-in-chief	61,000
Generals	1,275
Colonels and majors	433
Captains	90
Junior officers	35
Sergeants	19
Corporals and privates	2.5

▲ The final charge at Waterloo

Study 7

Use your imagination

1 After the Battle of Waterloo a British soldier wrote home to his father describing the battle, saying that he had lost three fingers. He said it might have been worse—he could have lost his head.

Write the letter that Captain Mercer might have sent to *his* father, describing what he did, saw and felt at Waterloo.

Mention:
> how long the battle lasted,
> why the artillerymen were exhausted, grimy and thirsty by the time the battle ended,
> the men and horses that Mercer saw after the battle.

(Think of a time when you were frightened, and how you tried to sound unconcerned when you told your parents about it later.)

2 In his novel *Vanity Fair*, William Thackeray describes how the soldiers' wives waited in Brussels while their husbands went to fight. Then 'wagons and long country carts laden with wounded came rolling into the town; ghastly groans came from within them, and haggard faces looked up sadly ...'

Describe how a soldier's wife waited in Brussels, hearing that first one side, then the other, was winning the battle, and at last saw her husband returning, wounded.

(Think of a time when you were anxious about someone and were waiting for him or her to come home safely.)

3 On Wednesday 21 June 1815, a newspaper called *The London Morning Post* announced:

'Defeat of Bonaparte by the Duke of Wellington

We yesterday had the supreme happiness of announcing ... the defeat of Bonaparte ... by the great and illustrious Wellington, his country's first pride and boast ...'

Write an account of the Battle of Waterloo as it might have appeared in a British newspaper in June 1815.

Mention:
> the French cavalry attacks on the British squares,
> the French infantry attacks,
> Napoleon's retreat when he heard that the Prussians were on the way.

(Think of a time when you and everyone you knew was relieved and delighted to hear that the side you supported had won a victory.)

Study 8

Major Percy brings the news to London

▼ Major Percy's journey

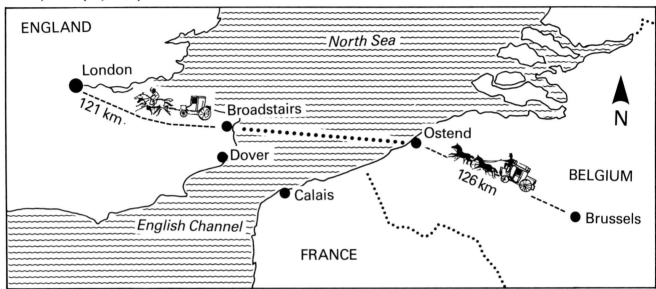

At the beginning of the eighteenth century, travelling in Britain was difficult and uncomfortable, but by 1815, the main roads had been improved. Travellers could cover long distances quickly instead of struggling through mud in the winter, or bumping over rough surfaces in the summer.

Major Percy, who brought the news of Wellington's victory to the British Government, left Brussels on the morning after the battle and reached London at midnight on 21 June. With him he brought two magnificent standards, each topped with a metal eagle, that had been captured from Napoleon. When the crowds in London saw the standards sticking out of the window of Major Percy's post-chaise (see below) they let out a great cheer.

◀ A post-chaise—a light carriage that could travel very quickly

A section through an eighteenth-century road designed by Thomas Telford. The road was firm because it was made up of graded layers of stone. Rainwater drained from the *cambered* (curved) surface into the ditches on each side ▶

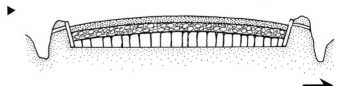

The British Empire after the French Wars

Conquered colonies

During the French Wars, the British Navy captured several colonies belonging to France and its allies. When peace was made in 1815 Britain handed some of these back, but kept the rest (see the table below). As a result of these gains, Britain's position in the world was much stronger, and the whole shape of the Empire had changed.

Territories gained by Britain 1783 – 1815

Date	Territory	Taken from
1788	Australia	Aborigines
1794	St Lucia	France
1795	Cape Colony	Holland
1795	Ceylon (Sri Lanka)	Holland
1796	British Guiana	Holland
1797	Trinidad	Spain
1798	Honduras	Spain
1800	Malta	France
1802	Tobago	France
1810	Mauritius	France
1810	Seychelles	France
1815	Ascension	France

In the eighteenth century, the most important parts of the Empire—the American and West Indian colonies—lay to the west of Britain. But after 1815, most of Britain's Empire lay to the south and east, in Africa and Asia. British Governments were no longer so concerned with what was going on across the Atlantic.

India

There had been British trading-posts in India since the early seventeenth century. These were set up by the East India Company, a trading company founded by Queen Elizabeth I in 1600.

During the Seven Years War, British forces in India had captured French trading-posts and taken over land belonging to Indian princes allied with the French. Between 1786 and 1805 the British conquered more territory, and made alliances with many Indian princes. They now controlled more than half of India.

The British needed to protect ships travelling between Britain and India. To do this they kept a string of colonies along the route. Trading ships were now always within reach of a British base, and could be protected from attack throughout the voyage.

Some of the bases in the east began to trade with China. Cape Colony, on the tip of southern Africa, became an important possession in its own right, and as a result the British fought a number of wars against the Africans and the Dutch settlers there. (See 'Conflicts in South Africa' on page 79.)

Australasia

By 1815 Britain began to take over Australia and New Zealand. In 1768 Captain James Cook had set out on a voyage to explore the South Seas. During this voyage he mapped New Zealand for the first time, sailed round Australia, and carefully charted the coast of New South Wales.

The British did not send any settlers to New Zealand until 1840, but New South Wales was a different matter. English courts often sentenced criminals to be transported to the colonies. In the eighteenth century, many were sent to America. After 1783, when the American colonies became independent, this was no longer possible. So the Government decided to send the convicts to New

South Wales instead, hoping to establish a colony there which might provide Britain with timber and other naval supplies.

The first shipload of convicts arrived in New South Wales in 1788. They drove away or killed the Aborigines who lived in the area and built a permanent settlement at Botany Bay. British courts continued to send convicts to Australia until 1867. In all, about 162,000 prisoners made the trip. Some returned home when they had served their sentences, but many stayed behind, married other convicts or free settlers, and settled in Australia for good.

Emigration after the French Wars

Between 1750 and 1850 the population of England, Wales and Scotland rose from seven and a half million to nearly twenty-one million. To feed this increasing population, British farmers had to produce more. They enclosed the old open fields and commons with hedges or walls, grew new crops, and bred healthier, heavier animals. In the Highlands of Scotland the landlords turned the people off the land and enclosed it to make sheep-runs. The Highlanders were left homeless and unemployed.

When the Wars with France ended, the British Government encouraged people who had worked on the land to emigrate to Canada. The Government paid their travelling expenses, gave them land to settle on and money to buy farming equipment. Many of the emigrants under this scheme were Highlanders.

▼ Captain Cook admired the Aborigines, but many settlers thought they were primitive savages. Most of the Tasmanian Aborigines were killed by British settlers

During the nineteenth century many workers left Britain to settle in America and the colonies of the British Empire, and English was spoken in every continent.

Study 9

Britain's Empire after 1815

1 Draw the map of the British Empire in 1815 opposite.
  (a) By 1815, was most of Britain's Empire in
       America and the West Indies,
       Africa and Asia?
  (b) Which country was Britain's most important possession?
2 The British needed a strong navy to guard the sea-routes to the countries in their Empire, and also bases for the ships that used these routes.
  (a) Give an example of a base that was used by ships travelling to and from India.

  (b) What did the British hope to gain from New South Wales that would help them to build up the Navy?
3 Give an example to show that Britain's new Empire
       caused wars between the British and the inhabitants of the Empire,
       was used by the British to get rid of people they did not want in Britain.

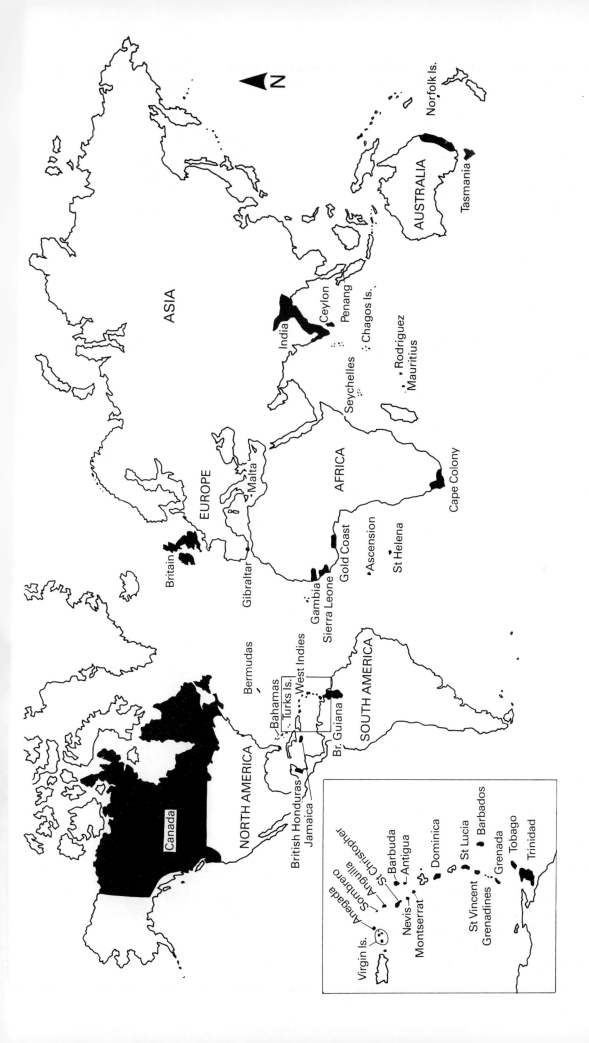

NORTH AMERICA

Canada

Bermudas

Bahamas
Turks Is.
West Indies
British Honduras
Jamaica

Br. Guiana

SOUTH AMERICA

EUROPE

Britain

Gibraltar
Malta

AFRICA

Gambia
Sierra Leone
Gold Coast

Ascension
St Helena

Cape Colony

ASIA

India
Ceylon
Penang

Chagos Is.

Seychelles

Rodriguez
Mauritius

AUSTRALIA

Tasmania

Norfolk Is.

N

Virgin Is.

Anegada
Sombrero
Anguilla
St Christopher

Nevis
Montserrat

Barbuda
Antigua

Dominica

St Lucia
Barbados

St Vincent
Grenadines
Grenada

Tobago
Trinidad

▲ The British Empire in 1815

Further work

Writing

1 Write a sentence about each of the statements below, saying whether it is true or false, and giving reasons for your answer.

> The only soldiers who succeeded in defeating Napoleon's armies were British.
>
> Some Scotsmen and Irishmen were better off in the Army than at home.
>
> Britain had less power overseas at the end of the Wars with France than at the beginning.

2 (a) Write brief notes explaining why the British
   (i) declared war on France in 1793 (page 56),
   (ii) sank the Danish fleet in 1801 (page 56),
   (iii) issued the Orders in Council in 1807 (page 71).
  (b) Using only your notes, write a paragraph on 'Trade and the Wars with France'.

3 The picture of *The Third of May, 1808* on page 67 and the picture of *The Battle of Waterloo* on page 72 both show an artist's idea of what happened on these occasions during the Wars with France.
  (a) Choose a man shown in one of the pictures and write one or two sentences saying what he appears to be doing and thinking.
  (b) What do you think the artist who painted the picture was trying to show about (i) the event he is illustrating, (ii) any war at any time?

Drawing

1 The names of many inns in Britain remind us of the Wars with France. Draw a sign for one or more of these inns:

   The Victory   The Battle of Waterloo
   The Jolly Sailor   The Volunteer

2 The lines below are from a song about a woman who was afraid that the Press Gang would seize her husband:

> 'If they take thee, Geordie, who's to win our bread?
>
> Me and little Jacky: better off be dead.'

Copy the words and illustrate them.

3 Draw a cartoon that might have appeared in a British newspaper in about 1816, encouraging unemployed British farm-workers to emigrate to Canada on government grants.

Drama

In groups of five:

1 Prepare a two-minute mime on one of these themes:

   On board a man-of-war
   Women and war
   On the battlefield
   After the Wars

2 Choose four groups to perform their mimes in front of the class.

Figure it out

Look at the table of prize money paid to British soldiers after the Battle of Waterloo on page 72. Was the prize money of the commander-in-chief roughly equal to that of

   3,000 privates,
   30,000 privates,
   300,000 privates?

▲ A man and a woman wearing clothes that were fashionable in 1815

4 Conflicts in South Africa

Trichardt's trek

Louis Trichardt was a Boer. The Boers were farmers whose ancestors had come from Europe to settle in South Africa. Most of them were of Dutch descent. In 1835 Trichardt was preparing to move from his home on the banks of the Indwe River. He wanted to escape from the British, who had already taken over the whole of Cape Colony further south, and were now moving north into Kaffirland where Trichardt and his family lived.

Trichardt hated the British. So he and his family decided to move north into unknown territory, well away from the British, and begin a new life where they would be free to do as they liked.

Several other families decided to go with Trichardt, and in May 1835 they set out with nine ox wagons packed with their belongings—furniture, tools, clothes, food, cooking utensils and boxes of bullets and gunpowder. They had a few horses, a herd of about 500 cattle, and flocks of sheep and goats.

Trichardt on the trek

Every day they travelled about 8 km across the high South African plain. They rose before it was light. The men harnessed the oxen to the wagons, and the women prepared breakfast. The children had lessons in reading and writing from a schoolmaster who was travelling with them.

Soon after it was light they set off. A few men armed with guns went ahead to explore the route on horseback. The other men drove the creaking ox wagons, while the women and children kept the cattle and sheep moving along.

When they had travelled far enough for the day, they stopped to allow the sheep and cattle to rest and feed on the grass of the plain. The animals needed plenty of rest and food to keep them healthy. Meanwhile some of the men went off on horseback to look for wild animals, such as deer or antelope, to shoot for their supper.

Every week or so, when they came to a place where the grass was especially good, they stayed for two or three nights to let the animals eat as much as they wanted, while the men checked and

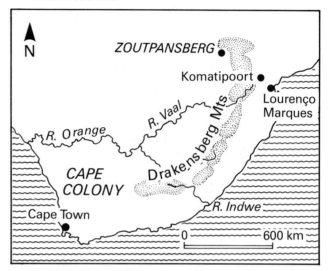

▼ Trichardt's trek

repaired the wagons. At first they held a service every Sunday, but after a few weeks they lost count of the days.

In December they reached the banks of the Orange River. They found a place where the water was shallow, and drove the wagons and the animals across. Then they pressed on. They tried to avoid areas where they knew African peoples lived, but further north, shortly after they crossed the River Vaal, they saw African villages which had been burnt down and the remains of human skeletons. The Africans had been at war with one another.

Zoutpansberg

After nearly a year's travel, Trichardt and his party reached an area far to the north, called Zoutpansberg. Most of the trekkers pressed on, but Trichardt saw that the grazing was good, there was plenty of water, and there were many deer and antelope to shoot. So he and a few others decided to settle there with their families. They built houses and a small hut to serve as a school. They also laid out gardens, and supplied them with water through a system of dams and ditches.

At first, life in Zoutpansberg was good. The cattle and sheep settled down well, and crops

A wagon being pulled up a steep river-bank. There were no bridges over the rivers in South Africa

were plentiful. The Africans who lived in the area seemed friendly. Trichardt usually let them come to the settlement to trade, but he would not allow them to approach if they were armed, or let them sleep anywhere near.

But Zoutpansberg was a lonely place. In June 1836 a party of Boer farmers on their way north visited the settlement, but as a rule Trichardt's party never saw any other white people. Soon they ran out of coffee and tea. Their clothes wore out. Then they began to run short of bullets and gunpowder. This alarmed Trichardt. Boers depended on their guns to hunt game for food, and to protect themselves and their flocks from attack. So Trichardt had to get powder and shot from somewhere.

▲ Two prosperous Boer farmers return from a day's hunting. A black servant carries one of their guns, and one of the animals they have shot

Trichardt's letters

Trichardt knew that there was a Portuguese settlement at Lourenço Marques, 400 km away on the coast, over the Drakensberg Mountains. In March and April 1837 he wrote two letters to the Portuguese governor, offering to trade cattle and animal hides in exchange for gunpowder. Visiting traders promised to see that his letters were passed on to the Portuguese, and in due course one of them was delivered.

Trichardt's letter was written in Afrikaans, a Dutch dialect spoken in South Africa. No one at Lourenço Marques could understand it, but the governor realised that Trichardt needed help. So he sent an African guide to Zoutpansberg to bring the trekkers down to the coast.

Trichardt leaves Zoutpansberg

When the guide arrived, Trichardt knew that he and his companions would have to abandon their trek and go with him. Their gunpowder had nearly all run out, and in any case life at Zoutpansberg no longer seemed so good. Some of the settlers had fallen ill with fever, and many of their horses and cattle were also sick. So they packed their wagons, and set out on the long trail over the Drakensberg Mountains to Lourenço Marques.

It was an adventurous journey. In places they had to cut a road across the hillsides. The eastern slopes of the Drakensbergs were too steep for the oxen to draw the wagons in the usual way. To stop the wagons running out of control they had to remove the rear wheels and drag them down like sledges.

As they wound their way down towards the sea, the climate grew hotter, wetter and less healthy. By the time they reached Komatipoort, where they could obtain food and medicine, several people and many cattle had died.

The end of the trek

The survivors pressed on. Eight months after leaving Zoutpansberg they reached Lourenço Marques. But most of them were ill with malaria and sleeping sickness. More people died, including Mrs Trichardt, and a little later, Trichardt himself.

Eventually all the men died except for Trichardt's son. In 1839 a ship called at Lourenço Marques, and took the survivors back to the south, where they could be sure of finding friends. Trichardt's trek had ended in disaster.

▲ Three Boer women dressed in the kind of clothes worn by nineteenth-century trekkers

How do we know?

Louis Trichardt's journal

When Louis Trichardt died in October 1838, the survivors of the trek found a journal among his belongings. The dates in the journal showed that Trichardt started it when he set out on the trek, but had not written much in it until July 1836. After this he kept it up until five months before he died.

The journal told the survivors what Trichardt had done and thought, but to them, it was more than an account of one man's life on the trek. It reminded them of what had happened in their own lives at that time, and they remembered moments of danger, or unexpected happiness, and small incidents that were not really important but which had meant a great deal to them.

1 Between what dates did Trichardt make the most entries in his journal?
2 From the information given in the story, where was Trichardt when he began to write regularly in his journal?
3 Which of these parts of the trek would you expect the journal to tell you least about?
    The trek to Zoutpansberg,
    The settlement at Zoutpansberg,
    The trek from Zoutpansberg to Lourenço Marques.

What do you think?

Trichardt's journal tells the story of a disaster. Why do you think the people of a country wish to remember the disasters in their history as well as the successes?

Trichardt's Monument

The Transvaal is one of the states of modern South Africa. A motorway runs through it, linking the towns along a line from the Vaal River in the south to the Limpopo in the north. A motorist travelling along the road can cover the distance between the two rivers in a day.

Many travellers along the motorway stop on the rocky plateau outside Pietersburg and look across to the high peaks of the Drakensbergs in the distance. In 1838, somewhere near here, Trichardt's wagons struck eastward, making for the mountain passes that would lead them to the coastal plain.

A memorial to Trichardt stands near the road. On its side a map, engraved in bronze, shows the route that the trekkers took from Zoutpansberg to Lourenço Marques.

1 When did Trichardt's trek cross the Vaal River?
2 What information given on the Monument helps to confirm that the trekkers left Zoutpansberg for Lourenço Marques?
3 Why was the Monument built at the spot where it stands?

What do you think?

Monuments are to remind us of events that happened in the past. Would it matter if we did not know what happened in the past? Give reasons for your answer.

Glossary

Use your own words to explain what each of these means:
      Boer   trek   journal

Understanding what happened

1 (a) In what year did Trichardt and his followers first leave Kaffirland?
  (b) Why did they leave Kaffirland?
  (c) Complete the sentence opposite by copying the statement that you think is correct:

By the end of 1839 most of the Boers who left Kaffirland with Trichardt had
    decided to settle in Lourenço Marques,
    died of sickness,
    returned to Kaffirland.

2 (a) Make a list of the supplies and possessions that the Boers
  (i) took in their wagons,
  (ii) herded alongside their wagons.
  (b) The Boers needed a constant supply of bullets and gunpowder.
  (i) Why did they need gunpowder?
  (ii) From which town did Trichardt hope to obtain new supplies of gunpowder?
  (c) Give two reasons why it was hard for the Boers at Zoutpansberg to get in touch with the Boers on the coast.

3 (a) The Boers took about a year to reach Zoutpansberg. Give two reasons why they saw so few Africans on their journey.
  (b) (i) How did the Africans in Zoutpansberg show they were not hostile to the Boers?
  (ii) How did the Boers show that they did not trust the Africans completely?
  (c) How did the African traders who passed near Zoutpansberg help the Boers?

Further work

Writing
1 Write three or more entries for a journal that a man or woman who went with Trichardt might have written during

    May 1835   June 1836   March 1837
2 Write the letter that Trichardt might have sent to the governor at Lourenço Marques, telling him about Zoutpansberg and suggesting that the two settlements might trade with each other.
3 Write an article that might have appeared in a newspaper in Cape Town in 1838, giving the news that Trichardt and a few survivors of the trek had arrived in Lourenço Marques.

Drawing
1 (a) Draw the map of Trichardt's trek on page 79.
  (b) Why did Zoutpansberg seem a good place to settle?
2 (a) Draw the picture of the Boer women on page 81.
  (b) Give an example of work done by women when the wagons were on the move.

3 (a) Draw a set of pictures telling the story of Trichardt's trek.
  (b) Write a caption to go with each picture.

Drama
In groups of four:
1 Louis Trichardt has called three Boers to a meeting to tell them that they cannot stay at Zoutpansberg, because their supplies are running out. Choose one of the following people each, and write the conversation that might have taken place between Trichardt and

        Conrad Pretorius, whose daughter is sick with fever,
        Peter Strydom, whose eldest son has just died,
        Hans Albrecht, whose wife has just had her first baby.
2 Give everyone at least four things to say.
3 Rehearse your scene in your group.
4 Choose two groups to perform their scenes to the class.

The Dutch colony

The Dutch come to South Africa

Dutch settlers first went to the southern tip of Africa in the middle of the seventeenth century. They set up a base where their ships could call on their way from Europe to the Dutch colonies in the East Indies. Some of them set up businesses supplying and repairing the ships which called in. Others wanted to farm, and by the end of the eighteenth century there were hundreds of Boer families like Trichardt's in South Africa.

The Boer farmers' life

Most Boer families lived on isolated farms of about 2,500 ha. They ploughed one or two hectares to grow crops, and used the rest to graze herds of cattle and sheep. They kept black servants to do the heavy work, such as carrying the water and rounding up the herds. When the Boers were not busy running the farm, they went out hunting on horseback. Sometimes they hunted springbok, which ate grass needed by the cattle. Sometimes they joined their neighbours to go hunting for the lions which preyed on their herds. The women stayed at home, did the housework and looked after the domestic animals.

The Boers were skilled horsemen. Their horses were hardy and patient. They could trot more than 80 km in a day, and could stand perfectly still while their riders took aim and fired muskets from the saddle. The Boers were good shots, and most of the meat they ate came from the animals they killed. They did not like to eat their sheep and cattle. They preferred to sell them.

Boer homes

Boer families had simple homes. Some spent months living in wagons or tents. When they built a house they generally made the walls from turf, and thatched the roof with reeds or grass. Their houses had two rooms. One served as a storeroom, kitchen, dining- and living-room. The other was the family bedroom.

They furnished the kitchen with a plain wooden table, some hard chairs, a few stools, and a couple of huge wooden chests to store things in. They had iron cooking-pots and tin plates. In the bedroom they had rough wooden bedsteads with leather thongs strung across them to serve as a mattress.

Boer wagons

A Boer family's most precious possession was its wagon, which was used as a kind of mobile home when exploring the countryside or visiting a distant market. It was long and narrow, with four heavy iron-shod wheels. A dozen semi-circular hoops were fixed along its length to support its canopy. This was made of thick canvas, painted on the outside to make it waterproof.

Teams of oxen pulled the wagons along at about 5 km per hour. On level ground, eight oxen could tow a lightly-loaded wagon, but if the country was hilly and the wagon full, a team of sixteen might be needed. The driver sat on a box at the front of the wagon and controlled his team with a long whip. A skilled driver could hit any one of the sixteen oxen without touching the others. A wagon on the move was an impressive sight, with the oxen straining to pull the lurching, creaking vehicle along in a cloud of dust, while the driver shouted and cracked his long whip.

The Boers' daily life

The Boers lived a simple life. Their food was plain, consisting mostly of deer-meat, mutton, mealbread, pumpkins and boiled corn, with tea and coffee to drink. They had few books, though every family owned a Bible which they studied carefully. They thought they had a lot in common with the tribes of Israel in the Old Testament, who had wandered with their flocks in Palestine. They often felt lonely and isolated. They relied on wandering merchants or occasional visits to a market town to keep them in touch with the outside world and provide them with luxuries such as tea and coffee, and necessities such as cloth, guns, bullets and gunpowder.

Study 2

The Boers of Cape Colony

1 (a) Draw the diagram of a Boer farmstead below, leaving enough space around it for more notes.

▼ A Boer farmstead

Farmer, hunting

(b) Annotate your diagram by labelling the following things on it:
   - flocks of sheep,
   - herds of cattle,
   - fields of crops.

(c) Add these people to your diagram, showing them at work:
   - a Boer woman,
   - an African labourer.

2 (a) Draw the picture of a Boer farmhouse.

(b) Use the information given in the section headed 'Boer homes' opposite to help you
   (i) draw the groundplan of the rooms in a farmhouse,
   (ii) annotate your plan, showing furniture that might have been used in each room.

3 (a) Read the section headed 'Boer wagons' opposite and look at the wagon on page 80.

(b) Draw a picture of a Boer wagon and label the main parts.

(c) Write one or two sentences explaining why a Boer farmer needed at least sixteen oxen.

▲ A Boer farmhouse

The Boers move north

The end of Dutch rule

In 1795 the British, who wanted a safe harbour on the route from Britain to India, captured Cape Colony. In 1814 the Dutch agreed to let them keep it in exchange for £6 million compensation. So the Cape became British.

Officials and settlers from Britain went out to South Africa. They wanted their colony to be a safe, peaceful place. They did not want to upset the black Africans, who outnumbered the white settlers many times over.

The British knew that Boer farmers made their African servants work very hard. Some Boers, like many black African peoples, owned slaves. Many Boers had large families, and as their numbers increased they took land from the Africans to use as pasture for their flocks. But the British made new laws which gave all free black Africans the same rights as whites, and made it illegal for the Boers to take over their land. Then in 1833 the British Parliament freed all the slaves in countries that were British possessions (see 'The abolition of slavery' on page 47).

The Great Trek begins

When the British Parliament freed the slaves, many Boers (like Trichardt), decided to leave Cape Colony. They did not want to live in a country where black Africans were, as one farmer wrote, 'placed on an equal footing with Christians.' They thought it was 'contrary to the laws of God and the natural distinction of race and religion'. So in 1836 and 1837 parties of Boer farmers with their families and black servants packed their wagons, left their homes and moved slowly north out of Cape Colony.

Study 3

The British take over Cape Colony

1 Copy the time-chart opposite and fill in the gaps.
2 Write notes to show why
  the British wanted to control Cape Colony,
  the Boers took over more land,
  black Africans had the same legal rights as white people after 1833.
3 What do you think the Boers meant when they said that the abolition of slavery was 'contrary to the laws of God and the natural distinction of race and religion'? Give an example of something the Boers did that supports your answer.

Date	Event
1795	The _____ capture Cape Colony from the Dutch.
_____	Cape _____ and the Boers become part of the _____ Empire.
1833	The British free all the _____ in their Empire.
1836	Boer families leave _____ _____ and move north.

Conflict with the northern peoples

As the Boers moved north many of them came into conflict with two nations. In the west they met the Ndebele, led by Mzilikazi. In the east they found the Zulus, ruled by King Dingane.

These two nations were related, and were both famous for their skill and courage in battle. They fought on foot. Their principal weapons were short wooden clubs known as *knobkerries*, and sharp throwing-spears called *assegais*. To protect and camouflage themselves they carried large shields made of cattle hide, and in battle they hissed like snakes to frighten their enemies.

When the Zulus and the Ndebele heard that the Boers with their wagons, herds and guns, were invading tribal land, they sent out warriors to kill the invaders or drive them back. The Boers knew this might happen, and always had scouts on horseback riding ahead of the wagons on the lookout for bands of warriors.

War on the trek

When a Boer scout saw a band of African warriors, he rode back as fast as he could to warn the rest of the trekkers. Most of the men then seized their guns, and rode out with him towards the Africans. When they were about 200 m away they stopped, their guns at the ready. If the Africans attacked, they waited until the nearest warriors were about 100 m away—too far to throw an assegai, but well within the range of the Boer muskets. Then they fired at the Africans, usually killing some of them, rode off a short distance, reloaded and waited again. Every time the warriors attacked, the Boers did the same, gradually falling back towards their wagons.

Meanwhile the women, the children and a few of the men who had stayed with them, had unyoked the oxen and dragged the wagons into a circle. They lashed them together, and filled any gaps with heaps of branches from thorn bushes. They called this ring of wagons a *laager*. They kept their horses in the middle of the laager, but there was no room for the rest of their animals.

When the Boers on horseback came in sight, the Boers in the laager pushed one of the wagons aside to let them in. Then they closed the circle, and waited for the black warriors to attack.

The men stood or crouched behind the wagons, their guns at the ready. The women stood beside them with spare guns and supplies of bullets and

▼ Photographs of Zulu warriors were sold to British troops as souvenirs

gunpowder. And all the time the warriors crept closer. At last they sprang upright and rushed towards the laager, brandishing their assegais. The Boers held their fire until the enemy were less than 50 m away. Then they fired. Their guns were loaded with special bullets which broke into four pieces as they flew through the air, so that one shot might kill or injure two or three warriors.

When each man had fired, he handed his gun to his wife to reload, took a loaded gun from her and was ready to fire again. The black warriors stood no chance. They never got close enough to injure the Boers. Some threw their assegais at the wagons, but these only bounced off the heavy canvas covering. At last they retreated, leaving their dead round the laager. In flat open country, a man on horseback with a gun could always defeat a spearman on foot.

▼ Boers defending a *laager* from attack. (A contemporary drawing)

The Ndebele retreat

In 1837 the Boers sent a small expedition to attack Mzilikazi's headquarters at Kapain. In nine days' fighting the Boers killed hundreds of Ndebele, and captured 7,000 cattle, without losing a man or a horse. Mzilikazi could see no point in fighting any longer. Instead he and the Ndebele people retreated north, leaving their lands to the Boers. The Boers called part of their new country the Orange Free State.

Study 4

The Orange Free State

1 (a) Draw the map of Natal, Transvaal and the Orange Free State opposite.
  (b) Why did the Boers feel more free in their new state than in Cape Colony?
2 Draw a picture to illustrate each of these statements:

   The Boers' wagons shielded them from attack.

   Women and children helped the men to defend the laager.

3 (a) Draw the picture of the Zulu warrior on page 87.
  (b) Would you expect the Zulus to have felt more or less threatened when the Boers set up the Orange Free State in 1837? Give reasons for your answer.

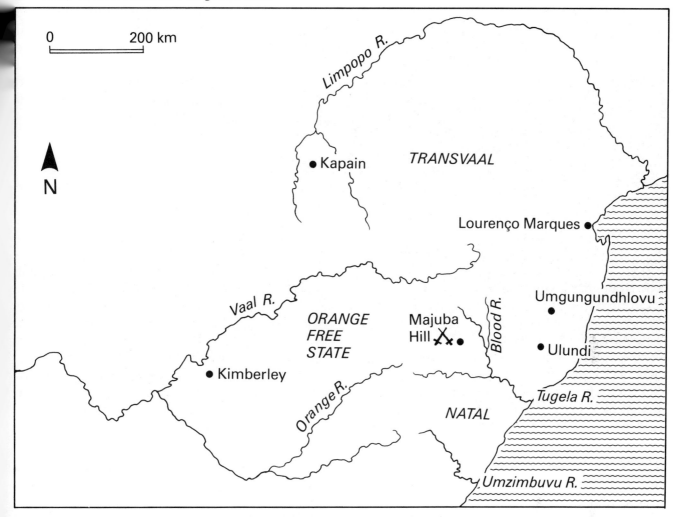

The Zulus fight back

In Natal, King Dingane and the Zulus also tried without success to drive the Boers back. Then in February 1838 Dingane invited a number of Boer leaders to come to his headquarters at Umgungundhlovu to make a treaty. Dingane and the Boers negotiated for four days. On the fourth day they signed a treaty granting all the land between the Tugela and Umzimvubu rivers to the Boers. Then Dingane invited the Boer leaders into his village for a drink of beer to celebrate.

Sixty-seven unarmed Boers went into the village. Dingane's warriors danced round them in celebration, and the King's servants offered them beer. Suddenly, Dingane shouted, 'Kill the wizards!' The warriors seized the defenceless Boers, dragged them to an execution stone, and beat their heads in.

Dingane's warriors left Umgungundhlovu and attacked all the Boer trekkers they could find in the area. The Zulus hoped that if they could kill a large number of Boers, as well as all their leaders, the rest would be so frightened that they would leave. At first it was easy for the Zulus because the trekkers were not expecting an attack. The first wagons the Zulus found were strung out across the plain, and could not be defended. They killed most of these trekkers, but a few escaped on horseback and warned others to be ready for an attack. This gave them time to prepare their laagers, and they drove the Zulus away. So Dingane's plan failed.

The defeat of the Zulus

The Boers were determined to have their revenge on Dingane. It was not easy, because the Zulus had learnt not to fight out in the open where horsemen had a good view and could gallop safely over the level ground. Instead they chose rocky, broken country where they could creep up on the Boers without being seen until they were close enough to kill them with their assegais.

So the Zulus gradually became more confident, and on 16 December 1838 the whole Zulu Army attacked a huge Boer laager commanded by Andries Pretorius. It was a fatal mistake. The Zulus attacked again and again. The men in the laager fired so many shots that they could hardly see through the smoke from their guns. 'It was all shouting and tumult and lamentation, and a sea of black faces,' said one of them afterwards. At last, after two hours' fighting, Pretorius ordered his men to charge. Three thousand Zulus were killed. Many lay dead in a nearby river, colouring the water red. The Boers named it Blood River.

The Boers settle in Natal

After the Battle of Blood River, Dingane and the Zulus left Natal, and Boer farmers settled there with their flocks. They needed workers, so they went to black villages and took boys away to work as 'apprentices' on their farms for a few years. Often the boys were orphans, and were treated little better than slaves.

Many Boer farmers in Natal found that their cattle were being stolen by black raiders. To prevent this the Boers gave their black servants passes to carry, and forced all other black people to leave the area around white farms. They also sent raiding parties to try to catch the thieves and bring the cattle back. On one of these raids the Boers attacked a village of the Baca people, killed thirty of them, and carried off 3,000 cattle and thirty apprentices. Yet the white men had no proof that the Baca had stolen their cattle.

The Boers leave Natal

In Natal there was a British settlement under the control of the Government in Cape Colony. The British thought the Boers were treating the Africans in Natal badly, and were afraid that this might lead to a war which would spread into Cape Colony. So in 1843 the British declared that the laws of Cape Colony applied in Natal as well. The Boers were furious. They had trekked to Natal to escape British rule. They attacked the British settlement, but fresh troops came from Cape Colony, and the Boers had to surrender.

Most Boers were still determined not to live under British rule. So once more they packed their belongings into their ox wagons and trekked away to the north and west across the River Vaal. Here they set up a new settlement, which they called the Transvaal.

Study 5

The Transvaal

1 (a) Copy the time-chart opposite.
   (b) Fill in the missing dates on your time-chart.

2 (a) Why, in your opinion did the Boers in Natal
       call the young Africans they forced to
       work for them 'apprentices',
       clear most Africans off the land around
       their farms?

3 Why did the Boers who left Natal in 1843 feel they had been betrayed by
   (a) the British,
   (b) the Zulus?

Date	Event
_____	Dingane murders 67 Boer leaders who have gone to his headquarters in Natal to make a treaty.
_____	Dingane leaves Natal after the Boers kill 3,000 Zulus at Blood River.
_____	The British take over Natal. The Boers leave and set up a new state—the Transvaal.

British rule in South Africa, 1833 – 1843

Discussion

1 *In pairs:* find two or more examples to support each of these statements:

Between 1833 and 1843

the British freed the slaves in Britain's African colonies and tried to live in peace with the tribes on the colonies' frontiers.

the Boers thought the laws passed by the British were destroying their way of life, so they trekked north to find new lands where they could settle.

many Africans were killed or driven from the lands as a result of their wars with the Boers.

2 With the help of the information that you have gathered, and any further facts that you can find, decide whether or not you agree with this statement:

'Between 1833 and 1843 the British caused more harm than good in South Africa and must take the blame for the suffering that happened there. They should not have interfered.'

You should be able to give reasons for your answer.

3 Ask one person to read his or her answer to the class. Do the rest of you agree?

The Zulu Kingdom

The Zulu economy

Zulu kraals

The Zulus lived on land bordering Natal and the Transvaal. Their way of life had not changed for hundreds of years. They lived in family groups. Each group consisted of a man, his wives and their children and servants.

Each family lived in a village called a *kraal*. Kraals were all built to the same pattern. In the centre there was an enclosure where cattle were kept at night. At one end stood the headman's hut. Beside it was his chief wife's hut. His other wives and their children lived in smaller huts which were set in order round the cattle-pen. The whole kraal was surrounded by a stout wooden fence set with thorns.

Zulu huts were round, made from a framework of flexible young branches hung with grass. A pole in the middle of the floor held the roof up. The hut had no windows, and only one doorway, just high enough to crawl through on all fours. The floor was made of clay and cow dung which made a hard, shiny surface. Near the centre of the

hut there was a stone hearth for the fire. Cooking-pots were made of clay. The family slept on grass mats which were rolled up during the day and hung from the wall on hooks.

Though the huts were dark and smoky, they had many advantages. They kept out the rain, were warm in winter, and cool in summer. They were also cheap and easy to build.

Zulu life

The Zulus spent most of their time out of doors. The men looked after the cattle, which were the family's most important possession. As a rule women were not allowed to enter the cattle-pen. They spent their time cooking, cleaning the huts, and growing maize and millet. When they had gathered the crops they were allowed to enter the cattle-pen to store the grain in holes in the ground.

Zulus had a healthy diet of milk, meat, fruit and grain. Each family was more or less self-supporting. They made their own cooking-pots

▼ Ulundi was the biggest *kraal* in Zululand, and the most important

and wooden plates, spoons and bowls. But most families had no blacksmith, and had to buy iron tools from a neighbouring kraal where there was a family which specialised in smelting iron.

Zulus had no money as we know it. Instead they exchanged some of their animals for the goods they needed. A man's wealth depended on how many cattle he owned. If he had a large herd he was rich and powerful. He could exchange some of the cattle to buy extra wives who would give him many children. The boys looked after the cattle, and when the girls married, their husbands had to make the chief a present of still more cattle. A few Zulu chiefs each had as many as seven or eight kraals with forty or fifty wives and more than 100 children. Some chiefs enjoyed themselves sitting in the sun watching their servants drive their herds of cattle past, counting how many they owned, and working out how rich they were.

The power of Cetewayo

Cetewayo, who became King of the Zulus in 1872, was the richest of them all. He had a dozen kraals, each with a hundred or so huts surrounding a cattle-pen which was so big that it was used as a parade ground for his army. The King of the Zulus had a huge number of servants. Every male Zulu had to leave home as soon as he was grown up and go to work in one of the royal kraals and fight for the king for as long as he was wanted.

As a rule the king kept the young men working for him for at least fifteen years. Until he let them go, they were not allowed to get married or set up home on their own. While they stayed with the king, the men learnt to fight, and occasionally went on expeditions against other tribes. A Zulu warrior did not consider he was a real man until he had 'washed his spear' in battle. In an emergency Cetewayo could call on 30,000 trained warriors to fight for him.

▲ This engraving of Cetewayo was published in *The Illustrated London News* in 1879

Study 7

Scenes from Zulu life, 1875

The first photographs were taken by a Frenchman called Aimé Laussart in 1840. A camera and the equipment that went with it were heavy, and it was impossible to take action photographs because the people who were having their photographs taken had to stand still for several seconds. Magazines and newspapers began to publish photographs, but they still relied on artists' drawings when they wanted a picture with action in it, or if they did not have a suitable photograph of a place that was in the news. An artist who worked for the newspapers usually had to rely on a written description of the scene he had been told to illustrate.

Drawing
In groups of four:
1 Draw a set of pictures that might have been used in about 1875 to illustrate an article on 'Scenes from Zulu life'.
2 Read the section headed 'The Zulu economy' on pages 91 to 92.
3 Draw one of these pictures each:
   a Zulu hut   a Zulu man at work
   a Zulu chief   a Zulu woman at work
4 Write a brief caption to go with your picture.
5 Mount your pictures on a large sheet of paper and display them.

The conquest of Zululand

The British invasion
Most white settlers in South Africa did not bother to try to understand the Zulu way of life. All they knew about the Zulus was that they could not read or write, wore hardly any clothes, and believed in ghosts and witches. They thought this meant that the Zulus were savages. Only a few white men really understood the Zulus. One was John Colenso, Bishop of Natal. He had learnt the Zulu language, and was friendly with Cetewayo. Bishop Colenso respected the Zulus, and thought they should be left in peace in their own country.

The British rulers of Natal disagreed. They wanted Cetewayo's land, and needed his people to work on their farms and help build a railway they were planning. They also feared Cetewayo's army. One of them wrote that Zululand was 'a source of perpetual danger to itself and to its neighbours'.

In 1878 Sir Bartle Frere, the British High Commissioner in South Africa, decided to take over Zululand. But he needed an excuse. So he wrote to Cetewayo ordering him to disband the Zulu Army. Frere knew that Cetewayo would refuse, and there were British troops waiting on the border to invade Zululand. They thought the invasion would be easy. The British had heard that some Zulu chiefs disliked Cetewayo, and would help them to depose him.

The defeat of the British
In January 1879 the Zulu King refused Frere's demands. Cetewayo was very angry, but he was also bewildered. The British had always been his allies. 'What have I said or done to the great house of England?' he asked. He got no answer. Instead three columns of British troops lumbered slowly into Zululand with their ox wagons. No Zulu chiefs came to help them, and on 22 January a Zulu army attacked one of the columns in its camp at Isandlwana, where it had stopped for the night. In all, there were 1,800 soldiers in the camp—950 British, and 850 black troops from Natal.

At first the British troops drove the Zulus off, killing hundreds of them with accurate rifle-fire. But soon the soldiers had used all the ammunition they were carrying. The rest was stored in strong boxes with the lids held shut by long screws. Some of the screws were rusty, and all of them were difficult to undo. So while the boxes were being undone the troops ran out of ammunition. Then the Zulus broke into the camp and massacred the soldiers with their assegais. Only 300 black

▼ A Punch cartoon: a Zulu teaches John Bull (standing for the British people) not to despise his enemies

Despise not your Enemy

A LESSON.

soldiers and fifty-five British escaped. But the Zulus had lost more than 2,000 men. 'There are not enough tears to mourn for the dead,' said Cetewayo when he heard of the battle.

After the British defeat at the Battle of Isandlwana, some of Cetewayo's chiefs tried to persuade him to invade Natal. Cetewayo refused. He did not want to take over any British territory. He only wanted the British troops to leave Zululand. So he attacked the other two columns, hoping to drive them back across the border. But he failed. The British riflemen drove the Zulus off.

The capture of Cetewayo

The British Government wanted revenge for the defeat at Isandlwana. It sent reinforcements to South Africa, and the troops advanced into Zululand. Many Zulu warriors had gone home. They were not used to fighting long wars. They carried very little food when they went to war, and had to go back to their kraals to get fresh supplies and to check that their cattle were safe.

The British continued to advance until they reached Cetewayo's kraal at Ulundi. They defeated the Zulus who were defending it, and burnt it to the ground. Cetewayo escaped, but a few weeks later he was captured. When the British commander, Garnet Wolseley, met him, he was impressed. He wrote that Cetewayo was 'quite the king in bearing and deportment'.

He sent Cetewayo into exile in Cape Town, divided Zululand into thirteen separate areas, and appointed a chief to rule over each. He shared out Cetewayo's cattle and wives between them. The thirteen chiefs were jealous of one another, and civil war soon broke out in Zululand. Meanwhile, in Cape Town, Cetewayo was trying to persuade the British Government to give him back his kingdom. He said he had done nothing wrong. 'I fought when I was attacked, just to ward off a falling tree, as it were, even as any other person would do. I ask you to look to my case and not to my colour.'

Cetewayo in Britain

Many British politicians sympathised with Cetewayo, and in 1882 they allowed him to visit Britain. He was very popular. Crowds gathered outside his hotel and cheered when he appeared on the balcony. He met leading politicians, and was even presented to Queen Victoria. He visited the Colonial Office and demanded to be allowed to go back to Zululand as king. But the British Government would only offer him half his kingdom. Britain would keep the rest.

Cetewayo was very disappointed. He said 'he had felt he was to be seated again. But the land which had belonged to his father was now very small ... and the idea of another piece of land being taken from that small country has buried him up to his knees again'. In the end he sadly agreed to accept what Britain offered, and sailed back to South Africa.

The death of Cetewayo

When Cetewayo reached South Africa a solemn ceremony was held to confirm him as king of the central part of Zululand. He seemed to have lost heart. But at the ceremony Hemulana, one of his chief ministers, complained bitterly to the British officials:

'You have taken the King's and the people's cattle and given them to those chiefs whom you set up. You have taken the royal girls and have given them to those chiefs of yours ... and given them the King's property. What is he to live upon? ... Do you mock us in saying you are restoring him? ... You are the author of all our troubles. Why don't you inquire about those kinglets of yours, those murderers? You have sent them away, and allowed them to keep all the King's property. ... We shall seize the cattle and stab those who keep them.'

Cetewayo's supporters began a war to win back his land and wealth from the other chiefs. But they were defeated, and in February 1884 Cetewayo suddenly died. A British doctor said he had suffered a heart attack. The Zulus believed he had been poisoned. Today nobody knows for certain how he died.

▼ The partition of Zululand

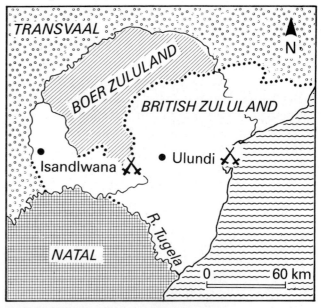

▲ Cetewayo went to a studio in London, and was photographed in formal European clothes

The Boers and the British take over

Cetewayo's followers were desperate. Their King was dead, and his enemies had invaded the land which the British had granted him. They needed help. They did not trust the British, so they turned to the Boers of the Transvaal. The Boers agreed to bring 'peace, law and order' to Zululand in return for being granted as much land as they considered 'necessary'. With the Boers' help, Cetewayo's followers defeated their enemies.

By the time the War was over, much of the Zulu Kingdom was like a desert. Because of the fighting, many Zulus lost their grain and cattle every year from 1879 to 1883. One chief told a British official, 'Unless help be given we must die. All our cattle and property have been taken from us ... weak persons and young children will by this time have died for want of ... food.'

In 1884 the Boers took a huge area of Zululand in the north for themselves. Finally, in 1887, the Boers and the British divided the rest of the Zulu Kingdom between them. 'It is dead,' a British official told a meeting of Zulus. 'It is like water spilt on the ground.'

Study 8

The end of the Zulu Kingdom

1 Copy the map of the partition of the Zulu Kingdom on page 95, and read the section headed 'The conquest of Zululand' on pages 93 to 96.

2 (a) Copy the quotation below:
'We shall seize the cattle and stab those who keep them.'
   (b) Who said the words above, and to whom did he say them?
   (c) The British had divided Cetewayo's land and cattle between thirteen chiefs. What happened to the Zulus who tried to win Cetewayo's property back again?

3 Copy the quotations below, and explain briefly what the British had done to the Zulus to make Cetewayo say what he did in each case:
   (a) 'What have I said or done to the great house of England?'
   (b) 'There are not enough tears to mourn for the dead.'
   (c) 'I ask you to look to my case, not to my colour.'

4 (a) Copy the quotation below:
'It is dead. It is like water spilt on the ground.'
   (b) Who said these words and to whom did he say them?
   (c) What had 'died' in 1887, and what did the speaker mean when he said, 'It is like water spilt on the ground'?

The scramble for Africa

Before 1875 only a very small part of Africa was under European rule. France controlled Algeria and Senegal, and Britain ruled South Africa. In addition, France, Portugal, Britain, Italy and Spain all had trading-posts scattered round the African coast. The rest of the continent was still ruled by African chiefs and kings. But between 1875 and 1914 European countries took over practically the whole of Africa.

Belgium was the first country to claim territory in the interior of Africa. In 1875 King Leopold II began to send explorers into central Africa. He set up a huge colony there to supply Belgium with rubber and ivory.

Rulers of other European countries saw what Leopold was doing, and also decided to take over territory in Africa. For example, between 1883 and 1885, Germany annexed South West Africa,

Togoland, Cameroon and German East Africa. Britain took over Egypt, Bechuanaland, Kenya and Rhodesia. The maps on page 98 show the African colonies owned by European countries in 1879 and 1914. Some of the Governments had no idea what to do with the land they claimed, but did not want to be left out of the scramble.

The Boer War

In 1886 gold was discovered in the Transvaal, and Africans who could no longer make a living from cattle and crops flocked to the mines, where they were employed to do the heavy work underground and at the pithead.

After the discovery of gold the Boers and the British in South Africa quarrelled. Sir Alfred Milner, the British High Commissioner in Cape Town, wanted to conquer the Boer republics of the Orange Free State and the Transvaal. He was supported by British businessmen who wanted to take over the Transvaal gold mines, which were the richest in the world.

The President of the Transvaal, Paul Kruger, was an old man. As a boy he had taken part in the Great Trek, and had been present at the Battle of Blood River. He was determined to defend the Transvaal against the British, and he used some of

▼ President Kruger of the Transvaal was a rough, uneducated farmer. But he was a skilful politician

▲ Diamond prospectors looking for precious stones. African workers dug out the soil and carried it over to the white prospectors, who sifted it to find the diamonds

▶ European possessions in Africa in 1879 (left) and 1914 (right). Some politicians drew the boundaries of their new colonies along lines of latitude and longitude. They often cut tribal lands in two, leaving half to be ruled by one power, and half by another

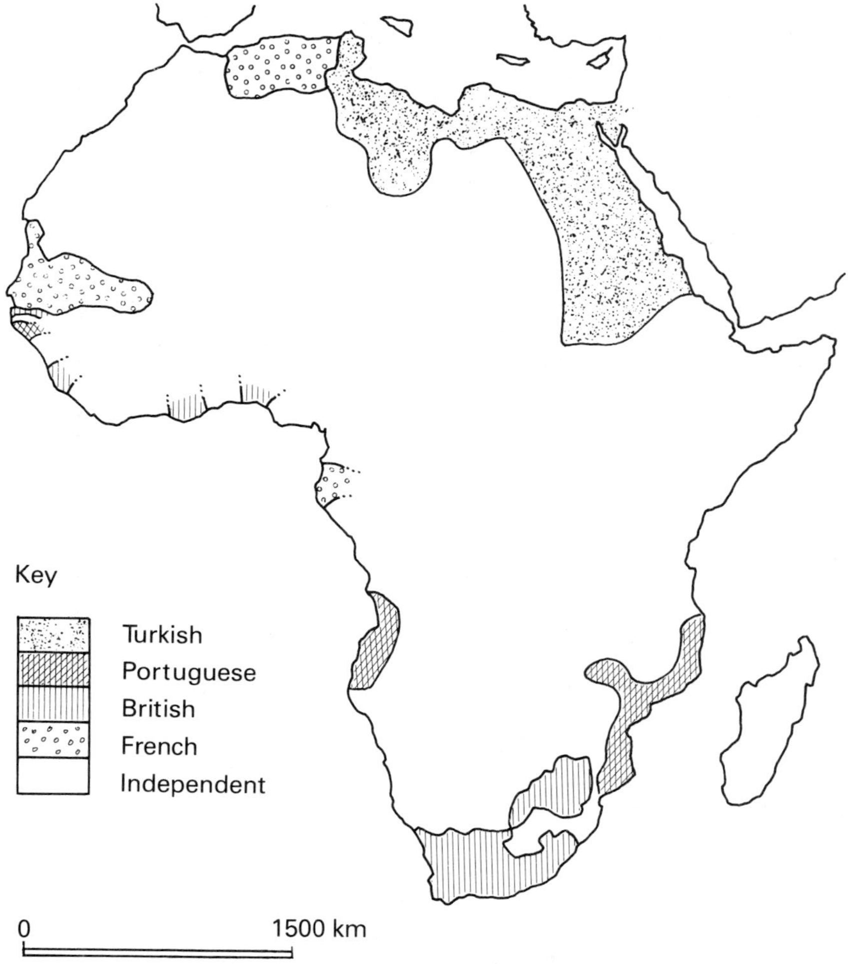

Key (left map)

Turkish
Portuguese
British
French
Independent

0 _____ 1500 km

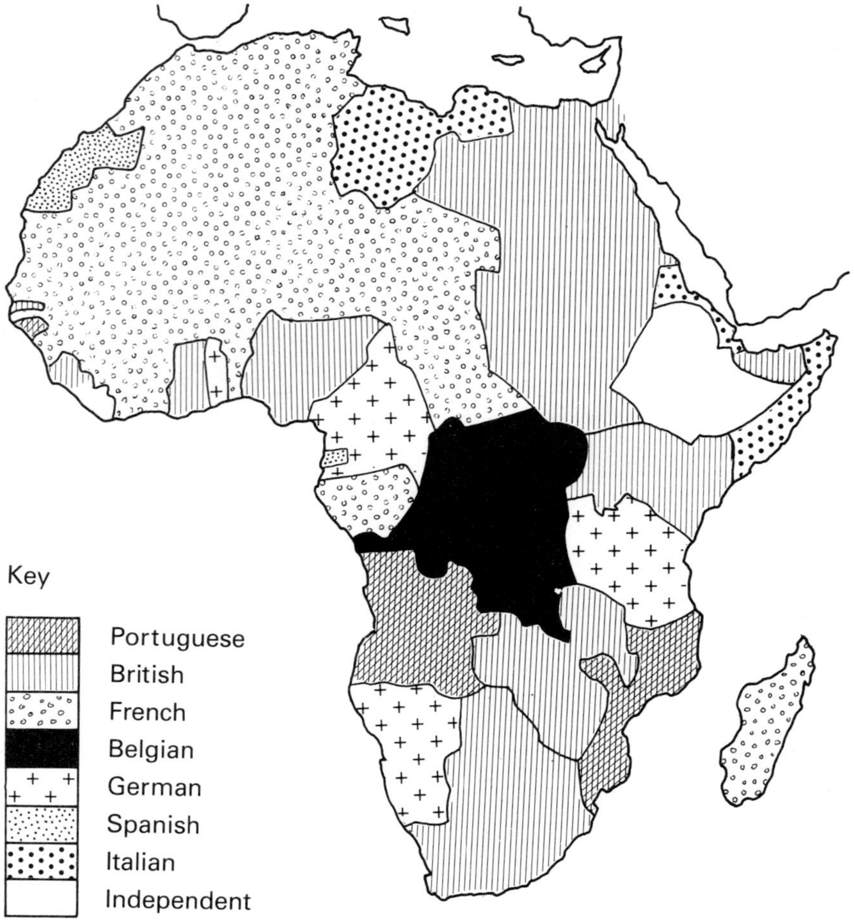

Key (right map)

Portuguese
British
French
Belgian
German
Spanish
Italian
Independent

the country's gold to buy modern weapons from Germany. In 1898 he purchased 37,000 Mausers, the most up-to-date rifles in the world.

The course of the War

War eventually broke out because of a quarrel over British subjects who were working in the Transvaal. The Boers were farmers. They did not know much about mining, so they had to allow the mining companies to employ British engineers and overseers. Though the Boers needed foreign workers, or *uitlanders*, as they called them, they would not give them the same rights as the Boer citizens of the Transvaal. For instance, Kruger refused to allow uitlanders to vote in Transvaal elections because he was afraid they would outnumber the Boers. Milner wanted an excuse to attack the Transvaal, so he insisted that Kruger should give the British equal rights with the Boers. Kruger refused, and war broke out in 1899.

Milner had thought it would be easy to defeat the Boers, but the well-armed farmers fought stubbornly. The War dragged on for three years before the Boers were forced to make peace with the British. In all 22,000 British troops, 35,000 Boers and 12,000 Africans died.

Study 9

Use your imagination

1 Lualana is a Zulu miner living in Johannesburg. Most of his family were killed in the Zulu Wars. Those who are left try to farm the poor land where the Zulus now live. Lualana's pay is low, and the hut he shares with some other miners is small and crowded. Write the answers he might have given to these questions in 1898:
   'What kind of work do you do?'
   'Why don't you go back to where you came from?'
   (Think of a time when you disliked the way you had to live but could not see how you could change it.)

2 Archie Maxwell is a British mining engineer living in Johannesburg. He thinks that the British would develop the wealth of the Transvaal much more efficiently than the Boers. Write the answers that he might have given to these questions in 1898:
   'Why do the Boers need British engineers?'
   'Why do you dislike Kruger?'
   'Why do you support Milner?'
   (Think of a time when you envied someone because he or she owned something that you thought you would make better use of.)

3 Hannah Kemp lives on a farm quite near to Johannesburg. Her parents trekked from Natal to the Transvaal in 1844 because they did not want to live under British rule. Her husband and the eldest of her four sons were killed when African tribesmen raided their farm in 1875. Write the answers that she might have given to these questions in 1898:
   'Why don't you trust the British or the Africans?'
   'Why does Kruger think the Boers need the weapons he is buying from the Germans?'
   (Think of a time when you found it hard to trust some of the people around you.)

4 Jefferson P. Rockwell, an American reporter, works for *The Philadelphia Chronicle*. In 1899 he is sent to South Africa to gather information for a series of articles on the situation there. When he arrives, it seems that war will break out at any minute, but he receives permission to interview Lord Milner and President Kruger.
   (a) Write three or more questions that he might have asked each man.
   (b) Write the answers that each of them might have given. (Remember that Milner was looking for an excuse to attack the Transvaal.)

South Africa in the twentieth century

In 1910 the Union of South Africa was set up, consisting of Cape Colony, Natal, the Orange Free State and the Transvaal. The Union was allowed to make its own laws, and in 1961 it became an independent republic. More than half of the white inhabitants of South Africa are Afrikaners—descendants of the Boers who believed that the black and white races ought to be kept apart. So under a system known as *apartheid*, the Government divided the country into black 'homelands', and areas for whites only.

White people have most of the good land and the rich industrial areas. Black men and women are allowed to work in white areas, but cannot make their homes there. They are only allowed to govern their own 'homelands', and have no say in how the Republic is governed.

In the 1980s the South African Government has had to start to change this system. But many black people believe they have a right to have a say in how the Republic is governed, and are prepared to fight for this.

Study 10

Black and white in South Africa

1 (a) Name the four states that formed the Union of South Africa in 1910.

   (b) In what year did the Union become an independent republic?

2 (a) What is the system called that divides South Africa into black and white areas?

   (b) Why did the majority of white people in South Africa approve of the system?

3 (a) Which people would you expect to have the higher standard of living, those in the black areas or those in the white areas? Give reasons for your answer.

   (b) The laws dividing black people from white were made by the Government of the Republic of South Africa. Why are black people unable to change these laws?

Study 11

London—capital of the Empire

By 1910, when the Union of South Africa was formed, the British Empire covered about a quarter of the world's land surface. London, the Empire's capital, was the largest and richest city in the world, and people belonging to the many different races and religions that made up the Empire could be seen in its streets. Wealthy Indians rode in carriages through the fashionable squares, and Asian and African seamen on shore-leave thronged the overcrowded alleys around the docks.

People from all over Britain came to London to look for work. It was said that more Scotsmen lived there than in Aberdeen, and more Irishmen than in

Dublin. The dairies in the city were often run by Welshmen. The poorest people lived in the crowded streets in the East End. Among them were many Jewish families, who had come to Britain from Eastern Europe, where they had been treated very badly.

In the countryside around London, where there was more space, builders were putting up rows of houses with gardens. The people who lived in these houses caught the morning train or travelled by underground to the offices and shops where they worked, and came home each evening to pleasant surroundings and fresh air.

→

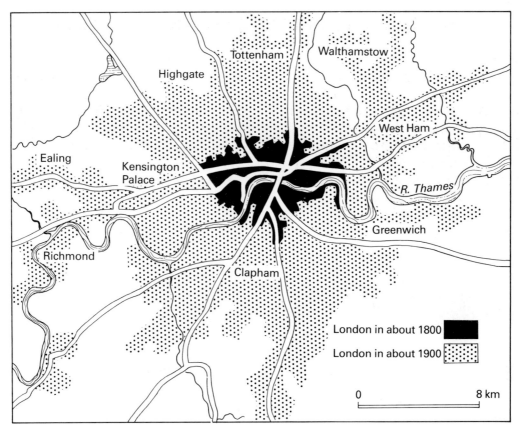

▲ During Queen Victoria's reign (1837 – 1901), the population of London and Greater London rose from just over 2 million to over 6.5 million

1 Look at the map of London above, and read the caption.
(a) How many people lived in London by 1901?
(b) Give two examples of places that would have been in the countryside in 1800 but which formed part of London by 1900.
2 Look at the picture of Rothschild Buildings opposite, and read the caption.
(a) What have the people in some flats done to try to improve the view from their windows?
(b) It was against the rules to hang anything over the balconies or on the staircase. What can you see that shows this rule was sometimes broken?

► This block of flats, called Rothschild Buildings, was named after a rich Jewish family who helped poor immigrants. Most flats had two rooms, a lavatory and a scullery. The rent was about £16 a year in 1910

▲ Houses were built in terraces to save land. The gardens were at the back. The rent for a house like these was about £30 a year in 1910

3 Look at the picture of terraced houses above, and read the caption.

(a) Compare the rent of one of these houses with the rent of the flat in Rothschild Buildings. Was it
   half as much,
   twice as much,
   three times as much?

(b) There are as many rooms at each front of the house as there are windows. How many rooms were there at the front of each house?

(c) Why was it a good idea to give the ground-floor room a bay window?

4 What information can you find in this study to support the following statements?

   At the beginning of the twentieth century, London was the capital of a great empire.

   People came from all over Britain and from foreign countries to settle in London.

   People who could afford to travel to their work were able to live in pleasanter surroundings than those who could not.

▲ A man and woman wearing clothes that were fashionable in about 1900

Study 12

One country—different races

Discussion

White Europeans have been settling in Africa and other parts of the world since about 1600. Since 1945, large numbers of Africans and Asians have come to live in Europe. Most people know someone who has emigrated or whose family has recently come to live in Britain. *You* may decide to settle overseas or work for part of your life in a foreign country, among people whose way of life seems strange to you. What answers would you give to these questions?

1 In many Islamic countries, such as Saudi Arabia, it is against the law to drink alcohol, and people think it is unclean to eat pork. To Hindus, cows are sacred animals, and in India they are allowed to wander in the streets. The Japanese sit on the floor to eat their meals. What may people from each of these countries find strange or off-putting about life in Britain?

2 If you found yourself living among people whose way of life was different from yours, which of the items below might you be
   (a) willing to change,
   (b) unwilling to change?
      style of dress,
      food and drink,
      religious practice,
      ideas about government,
      social customs, for example allowing women to eat with men, or expecting them to wait until the men have eaten.
Give reasons for your answers.

3 Ask one person to give his or her answer to the class. What do the rest of you think?

Further work

Writing

1 Copy the statements below and give two or more examples to illustrate each of them:

> The Boers, and the Afrikaners who were descended from them, disliked living under British rule and set up their own independent states.

> Quarrels among the Zulus helped the Boers and the British to take over their kingdom.

> The British realised that South Africa could become a wealthy country, and between 1878 and 1899 used excuses to take over land that did not belong to them.

2 Each of these men had to make important decisions that he knew would affect the lives of his people:

> Dingane   Sir Bartle Frere
>   Paul Kruger

(a) Choose one of these men and write brief notes saying
   (i) which people he belonged to,
   (ii) why he had to make one important decision and what he decided to do,
   (iii) what happened as a result of his decision.
(b) Use your notes to write a paragraph of four or five sentences about the leader you have chosen.

3 The South African way of life today is partly the result of the way in which white settlers found enough labourers to develop their farms and mines.
(a) Make brief notes on the ways in which these people found the workers they needed and how they treated them:

> settlers in Natal, 1838,
> mine owners in the Transvaal, 1870,
> people of the white areas in the twentieth century.

→

(b) Write the heading 'White employers and black labourers' and complete this sentence: 'In the nineteenth and twentieth centuries white people needed black labourers to work for them because …'

(c) Complete your essay by turning your notes into sentences.

Drawing

1 Draw a picture illustrating an important event in Boer history, that an Afrikaner boy or girl might have drawn in 1961 to celebrate South Africa's independence.

2 Draw one or more pictures under the title 'The British Army in Africa' that might have been drawn by a British boy or girl in 1899.

3 Draw a set of four pictures telling the story of Cetewayo. Give each picture a caption.

Drama

In groups of three:

1 The following people might have gone on the Great Trek, or might have attacked the trekkers:

> a Boer man or woman, aged 35,
> a Boer boy or girl, aged 10,
> a Zulu warrior, aged 20.

Twenty years later they might have been asked what they remembered about the Great Trek. Choose one of these people each.

2 Read the sections headed 'The Boers move north' and 'Conflict with the northern peoples' on pages 86 to 88.

3 Shut your book and write *not more than* five key words to help you with your answers to these questions:

> What do you remember most clearly about the Great Trek?
> Why do you remember this so clearly?

4 Using your notes, give your answers to the rest of your group.

5 Choose two or three groups to give their answers to the class.

Figure it out

We are told that

> 3,000 Zulus died in the Battle of Blood River in 1838,
> 1,445 British troops died in the Battle of Isandlwana in 1879.

Which of the figures given above would you expect to be a rough estimate and which would you expect to be an exact total? Give reasons for your answer.

5   The British in India

The Tirhut Famine of 1874

Kisch's circle

In 1874 Herman Kisch was twenty-three. He was the son of a London surgeon, and he had recently joined the Indian civil service. Every week he wrote to his family in London to tell them what he was doing. On 11 March he wrote that he was on his way to take charge of his 'circle'—an area of just over 500 sq. km at Tirhut, in Bihar, in the north-east of India, where there was a famine.

To help him govern this area Herman had three clerks, twelve sub-superintendents and twenty-four messengers. Inside his circle he was a very powerful man. 'I have full liberty to adopt whatever measures I think necessary,' he told his family. But every week he had to send a written report to his superior officer telling him everything he had done.

Famine in Tirhut

When Herman reached Tirhut he found that the Famine was very severe. A few months earlier the rains had failed, and now in many places there was no rice left. He visited one village and saw children so thin that they looked like skeletons. He wrote, 'Unless I had seen it myself I could not have believed that anyone could live with so thin a covering to the bones. The very colour of the bones was visible through the thin film that surrounded it.'

Relief work

With the help of the Indian Government, Herman immediately set to work to provide food for the people. First he set up storehouses—one for every ten villages—and appointed a salesman, two

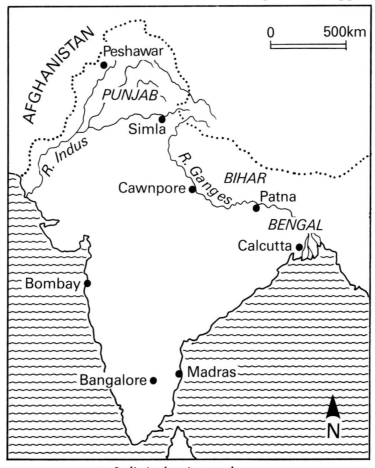

▲ India in the nineteenth century

105

▼ Most Indians lived in small villages. This drawing
was made by an Englishman working in India in the
nineteenth century

messengers and a watchman for each storehouse.
The authorities in other districts supplied him
with grain. 'All day long,' he wrote, 'rice is being
poured into my circle. Every day two or three
lieutenants, captains and majors come ... Each
officer brings perhaps 300 or 500 carts with three
to five bullocks each.' The carts carried rice from
the nearest railway line. Then Herman had to 'run
about like mad' to make sure that the rice was put
into the right storehouse.

If the people were too ill or weak to work, he
gave them free food from the stores. If they were
fit he found work for them damming rivers,
digging water-channels, building roads and
reservoirs and digging storage tanks. He gave
women cotton to spin into thread, or if they had a
loom, thread to weave into cloth. The Indian
Government paid the peasants for their work,
and they used the money to buy rice from the
nearest storehouse. Soon Herman was providing
work for 15,000 people, and giving free food to
3,000 who were unfit for work.

Inspecting the villages

Herman had to work very hard. He wrote:

'I am supposed to make myself personally
acquainted with the condition of every
village. Every day I have been from seven to
eight hours a day in the saddle, riding about
from village to village, and searching out
those who are able to work ... and those
who from weakness or disease can do no
work at all.'

Occasionally the Indians irritated him. In some
villages most of the people were *Brahmins*—
Hindu priests. Many were starving. Herman
wrote:

'If you ask one of these men what work he is
able and willing to do he answers that he can
pray. There is a great temptation to get into a
rage with this answer. But the Brahmin
would die without a murmur sooner than
work on a tank or road with common
coolies.'

Herman found that some store-keepers cheated. They claimed they had given out more free grain than they had done. They sold grain at a higher price than the one fixed by the Government. As there was never enough time to check the exact weight of grain delivered to them, they kept some rice for themselves. Whenever Herman discovered a dishonest store-keeper he had him put in prison. This did not have much effect. 'You can form no idea of the amount of swindling and robbery that goes on,' he wrote. But he was not surprised. The store-keepers were poorly paid, and had been appointed in a great hurry. Herman thought the people generally were not much worse than 'those of their education are in other countries'.

Visiting the government works

Herman also had to make sure the dams, roads and reservoirs were properly made. By the middle of May 1874, forty reservoirs were being built in his circle and he had to visit them all regularly. One day he was on horseback from eight o'clock in the morning till nine at night. He had two horses, but he was riding so far that they could not get enough rest and became 'rather weak'. He complained to his district officer, who sent him two more.

Paperwork

When he returned to his office after his tours of inspection, Herman had to write reports, send detailed orders to his sub-superintendents who were in charge of the relief works, and order tools, food and materials. He also had to record in his account book all the money he spent and received. Late one night he wrote home, 'Today from 6 a.m. till 12.30 p.m., with the exception of breakfast-time, I was doing my office work, and from 12.30 p.m. till 8 p.m. I was out on my horse.'

The end of the Famine

In June the rains came, but rice still had to be brought in while the new crop was growing. In July Herman wrote, 'If I stopped the sale of government grain for two weeks the air would be so foul with the dead that it would be impossible to move outside the house.' The rains ruined the roads. Bullock carts bringing in rice sank up to their axles in mud, and sometimes there was so much flood water that Herman could only get about his circle on a 'large elephant; a small one is no use'.

The rain ensured a good crop of rice, and the Famine ended. The rice brought in from other areas meant that hardly anyone had died of starvation. Herman was pleased, and he found that he had learnt a lot. He wrote:

'When I came to Tirhut I knew no more how to dig a good tank or build a grain store, or to store grain so as to avoid injury from damp or heat, or do a hundred other things that I have to do, than I have of how to build an English house or play the piano. Now I can do very well the things I have mentioned.'

Study 1

How do we know?

Herman Kisch's letters

When Herman Kisch died in 1945, his daughter collected the letters he had written home when he was a young man and published them in a book called *A Young Victorian in India*.

1 Give the dates of the first and last letters in which Kisch mentions the Tirhut Famine.
2 Roughly how many letters about the Tirhut Famine would you expect to find in *A Young Victorian in India*?

3 You will find several quotations from Kisch's letters in the story of the Tirhut Famine. Copy the statements below and add a quotation to illustrate each of them:

Herman Kisch worked hard to relieve the Famine.

More people would have died if he had stopped working hard.

The Hindu priests dealt with the Famine by following the teaching of their religion.

What do you think?
In order to study people and events in the past we need:

> *primary sources:* these are first-hand pieces of evidence which come from the actual time of the people and events, and
> *secondary sources:* these are pieces of evidence which come from people who were not there at the time.

Is *A Young Victorian in India* a primary source or a secondary source? Give reasons for your answer.

The Indian Famine Commission's Report
The officials of the Indian Famine Commission worked for the British Government. In 1881 they published a report which included a table of figures. It showed which areas of India had suffered from famine between 1769 and 1880, how long each famine had lasted, and the interval or length of time between outbreaks of famine. The figures in the table below are taken from that table.

1 Herman Kisch says that there was a famine in Tirhut in 1874. What are we told in the Report that confirms this statement?
2 (a) Was the famine of 1873 – 74 more or less severe than the one six years before?
  (b) Give an example of the work done by Herman Kisch that may help to explain *why* these famines were not equally severe.
3 In the story we are told about some documents that Kisch wrote that may have been used by the men of the Famine Commission to write their report. Which documents were they?

What do you think?
Are the figures in the Report likely to be reliable or unreliable? Give reasons for your answer.

Famines in Bengal
(The Tirhut Circle was in Bengal)

Date	Severity of famine	Length of famine	Interval
1865 – 1866	XXX	2 years	81 years
1873 – 1874	XX	1 year	6 years

XX = famine
XXX = severe famine

Understanding what happened

1 Copy the time-chart opposite and use these words to fill in the spaces correctly:
> reservoirs   rains   Circle
> harvest   storehouses   rice
2 (a) How did these people help Kisch in his work?
  Officers in the Army,
  Sub-superintendents,
  The district officer.
  (b) How did Herman Kisch help these people?
  Villagers who could work to buy rice,
  Villagers who were unfit for work.
3 (a) Copy the statement that you think is correct:
  The Famine was caused by lack of rain in the Tirhut Circle.
  The Famine was caused by lack of rice in the Tirhut Circle.
  (b) Give your reasons for choosing the statement that you have copied.

Herman Kisch and the Tirhut Famine, 1874

Date	Work done by Kisch
March	Kisch arrives in Tirhut to deal with a _____ famine.
April	Kisch builds _____, imports rice and makes sure the villagers of his _____ have enough food.
May	Work on forty _____ has begun. Kisch inspects the work.
June	The _____ begin. Kisch supplies the villagers with food until the next _____ .

Further work

Writing

1 Write the report that Herman Kisch might have sent to his superior officer at the end of his first week in the Tirhut Circle. Describe the effect that the Famine is having on the people in the villages and say what will be done to help them during the coming week.

2 Write an article that might have appeared in the Indian Famine Commission's Report of 1881. Explain what problems are caused by too much or too little rain, and suggest ways to collect and store water.

3 An officer in charge of a 'Circle' had to understand the people he governed, see what needed doing and make sure that work was carried out promptly and efficiently. Write the report that might have been written on Herman Kisch by his superior officer in 1874. Say whether or not Kisch has carried out his duties and give examples to support your opinions.

Drawing

1 (a) Draw the map of India in the nineteenth century on page 105.

(b) Which country governed India in 1874?

2 (a) Draw the picture of a hut in an Indian village on page 106.

(b) Give an example of something that a Londoner would have found strange about life in an Indian village.

3 (a) Draw a set of pictures showing three types of transport used in the Tirhut Circle, that might have been used to illustrate *A Young Victorian in India*.

(b) Write a caption to go with each picture.

Drama

In groups of four:

1 Write a scene in which Herman Kisch tries the case of a store-keeper who has been arrested for cheating. Choose one of the following people each:

Herman Kisch, the magistrate,

Sub-superintendent Das, one of Kisch's officials who arrested the store-keeper,

The store-keeper, who pleads not guilty,

A villager, who accused the store-keeper of charging more for rice than the price fixed by the Government.

2 Give each person at least three things to say before Kisch gives his verdict and pronounces the sentence.

3 Rehearse your scenes in your groups.

4 Choose two groups to perform their scenes to the class.

Glossary

Add these words to your glossary and explain, in your own words, what each of them means:

Circle   Brahmin

The government of India

Nineteenth-century India

In the second half of the nineteenth century, many young men like Herman Kisch left Britain and went to make a career in India. It was a vast country, much bigger than it is now. It included both Pakistan and Bangladesh. It had many different races of people, several different religions and hundreds of dialects. Large areas of the country were ruled by Indian princes. But they had all made treaties with the British, promising to do as the British wanted.

The Indian Mutiny

Ever since the British first set up trading-posts in India early in the seventeenth century, British India had been ruled by the East India Company. But in 1857 many of the Indian troops in the Company Army mutinied.

In most places the mutinies ended quickly, but in parts of the north, the Indian population joined the troops and attacked British officials and their families. At Cawnpore the local prince ordered that all the British, including women and children, should be killed, and they were murdered with horrifying brutality. When the Mutiny was over British troops took their revenge, killing mutineers without mercy.

The British Government was shocked by the Mutiny. It decided to abolish the East India Company and take direct control of India.

After the Mutiny

Many people in Britain thought the Indians ought to be punished for the Mutiny. The Government disagreed. It insisted that officials in India should work to improve the life of the people there. Queen Victoria agreed with her ministers. She took a great interest in India. As soon as the Mutiny was over she wrote that 'the Indian people should know that ... the greatest wish on their Queen's part is to see them happy, contented and flourishing'.

▼ Queen Victoria at her desk, with Abdul Karim beside her. (A photograph taken in 1895)

Victoria ordered her officials to allow all Indians complete religious freedom, and said that any Indians with enough ability should be given government jobs. An Indian Muslim, Abdul Karim, worked in her household in Britain, and tried to teach her Hindustani. Victoria thought her ministers were narrow-minded and snobbish in their attitude to Indians, and often complained that not enough Indians were given awards and decorations by the Government.

Study 2

The change of government

1 (a) Read the section headed 'The government of India' opposite.
   (b) Copy the notes below. Set them out in your notebook in the way you are shown here.

India in the nineteenth century
Country   included modern: India
                                      Pakistan
                                      Bangladesh
People   many: nationalities
                          religions
                          dialects
Rulers

   (c) Complete your notes by explaining why the Indian rulers obeyed the British.

2 (a) Copy the notes below:
End of company rule
East India Company ruled India from C7
1857: Indian troops in Company Army mutinied
Events of Mutiny

   (b) Complete your notes by writing briefly on what the Indians and the British did during the Mutiny.

3 (a) On a piece of rough paper, copy this sub-heading:
Government policy after the Mutiny
   (b) Write brief notes on
      British Government policy in India,
      Queen Victoria's attitude to India and Indians.
      Write each piece of information on a new line, so that you have a list.
   (c) *As a class:* choose three people to write their notes on the board. Are their notes
      brief,
      clearly set out,
      easy to understand?
      Choose the best set of notes and copy them into your notebook.

Test your memory
(a) Study your notes for five minutes.
(b) Shut your book and see how quickly and accurately you can write the notes you have learnt on a piece of rough paper.
(c) Compare the notes you have just made with those in your notebook and give yourself marks out of 10 for accuracy.

The viceroys of India

The viceroy was head of the British administration in India. He was appointed by the Government in Britain, and he ruled India with the advice of the two councils made up of Indian government officials and Indian princes. But if the viceroy liked, he could ignore the advice of his councils. He was much more powerful in India than Queen Victoria was in Britain.

The viceroy, attended by about 300 servants and soldiers, lived in Government House, a splendid mansion in Calcutta, built by Lord Wellesley at the beginning of the nineteenth century.

Part of Government House consisted of offices where the viceroy's ministers read reports and gave instructions which their clerks wrote out and sent to officials all over India. The rest of the building was taken up with the viceroy's private quarters and a number of huge, magnificently furnished state rooms. Here the viceroy entertained important visitors such as Indian princes, or ministers from other countries. Everything was done to impress guests with the power and wealth of the British in India. When an important visitor arrived in the grounds of Government House, he was greeted by a salute fired from a number of field guns, and soldiers in elaborate uniforms lined the pathways, stairs and corridors.

At formal banquets, scores of waiters and footmen in scarlet uniforms served the best food and drink that money could buy. The guests wore expensive, fashionable clothes and behaved very correctly, though on one occasion Lord Lytton, who was viceroy from 1876 to 1880, shocked many of his guests by smoking cigarettes between courses at a banquet. At formal balls a uniformed band provided the music, and the refreshments were always elaborate and expensive.

Even when there were no visitors the viceroy was not left alone. Lytton wrote:

'I sit in the privatest corner of my private room, and if I look through the window, there are two sentinels standing guard over me. If I go up and down stairs an a.d.c. [assistant] and three beings in white and red nightgowns with dark faces run after me. If I steal out of the house by the back door I look round and find myself stealthily followed by a trail of fifteen persons.'

Lytton disliked all the fuss and attention, but some viceroys loved it.

▼ Lord Lytton wearing his official robes

Study 3

The viceroys

Drawing

1 (a) Draw the viceroy, dressed in his official robes.
  (b) Whom did the viceroy represent in India, and who appointed him?
2 (a) Draw a picture of one of the viceroy's servants.
  (b) Copy what Lord Lytton said about his servants and attendants at Government House.

3 (a) Draw a picture to illustrate what happened when an important visitor arrived at Government House.
  (b) Write a paragraph describing Government House and the visitors the viceroy might have received there.

Study 4

Photographs of India

The British who lived in India at the end of the nineteenth century sent photographs as well as letters to their families in Britain. Today we use these photographs to illustrate history books (like this one). The photographs give us an impression of what life was like at that time in India—but it may be the wrong impression.

1 The Indians shown in Photograph A are *beaters*. The hunter had to know which direction the tiger would come from, so that when it sprang he could quickly line it up in the sights of his rifle and fire. The beaters' job was to drive the tiger through the undergrowth towards the hunter. It was dangerous work and the beaters risked being killed or maimed by the tiger.

(a) Which person in the photograph seems to have played the most important part in the hunt? Give reasons for your answer.
(b) Why do you think the woman was included in the photograph?
(c) Why do you think the photographer included the other people in the photograph?

▲ **Photograph A.** Tiger-shooting was a sport for the rich and famous. Here the Viceroy, Lord Curzon, poses with his wife beside a tiger he has just shot

2 When a photograph is used to illustrate a book, it may have to be trimmed to fit the space allowed for it. Look at Photograph B.
   (a) Why might it still be called *A Tiger Hunt*?
   (b) What important piece of information about tiger-hunting has been left out?
   (c) If you knew nothing about tiger-hunting, what impression might you form about the part played by the hunter, from looking at Photograph B?

3 In the nineteenth century, some Indian states were ruled by rich Indian princes. There were Indian lawyers and doctors in the cities. But most of the photographs the British sent home showed only those Indians who were servants.
   (a) Why do you think that most photographs sent home to Britain showed only those Indians who were servants?
   (b) Why are the photographs on pages 112 to 114 suitable for a chapter in a book about the British in India?
   (c) If you were writing a book called *India in the Nineteenth Century*, what kind of photographs would you look for? Give one or more examples.

▼ Photograph B

▲ An English gentleman being carried by his Indian servants in a palanquin

The Indian civil service

All the most important officials in India were members of the Indian civil service. There were just over a thousand of them. They were powerful men with secure, well-paid jobs, so whenever there were vacancies in the service there were plenty of applicants. Candidates for jobs had to take a special examination, usually at the age of eighteen. They could choose as many subjects as they liked from a long list which included English, Greek, Latin, French, German, Italian, Mathematics and Science. The candidates who scored the highest total of marks were offered the vacant places. Then they went to university for two years, and after this they were sent to India.

Wealthy Indians sometimes sent their sons to England to take the examination in the hope that they would be able to join the civil service, but not many succeeded. The examination favoured those who had been born and brought up in Britain. In 1870 only four Indians were members of the service, though thousands helped to run the country by working as clerks.

The Calcutta College

If a young civil servant was sent to Bengal province, he had to spend a few months at a college in Calcutta learning an Indian language. John Beames arrived there from England in 1858 and wrote an account of his life at the College. He lived in a boarding-house. He had his own bedroom, but shared a sitting-room with a fellow student.

Most mornings they got up about five, drank tea on the verandah, and then went riding until about seven. When they returned they drank more tea, smoked, read the papers and chatted with friends. At nine they had breakfast, which consisted of fish, mutton chops, curry and rice, bread and jam, and 'lots of fruit', washed down with red wine mixed with iced water. Then they studied for two hours. At noon they went out to pay calls on fashionable ladies, usually the wives and daughters of important officials whom they wanted to impress.

When they got back they had lunch, which Beames described as 'an elaborate meal of soup, hot meat, curry and rice, cheese and dessert', with wine and beer. After this heavy meal they slept for an hour or two. At five they went riding again, had dinner at seven and then went to bed.

Beames did not learn much at Calcutta, and was pleased when he was sent to a district in the Punjab on the other side of India as an assistant to the district officer. If he did his job well for a year he would be given a permanent post in the civil service. If not, he would be dismissed.

The work of a district officer

Each district officer controlled an area of about 11,500 sq. km—more than half the size of Wales. He had to collect taxes and act as judge in his district. He also had to hold village meetings to explain government policy to the people and make sure that they did as they were told. He had to spend three or four months every year touring his district. In remote areas the officer and his wife lived a lonely life, for there were few other British people, and they did not mix much with Indians. So a district officer and his family usually welcomed the arrival of an assistant.

The day after Beames arrived in the Punjab, his district officer showed him into a courtroom crowded with people, and then walked out, leaving him in charge. Everybody spoke in Punjabi, and Beames did not understand a word they said. So his clerk translated their evidence into Hindustani, which Beames had learnt. Beames wrote out a summary of the evidence in English, and at the end of each case he read it through to himself and came to a decision. He wrote afterwards, 'There was no law in the Punjab in those days. Our instructions were to decide all cases by the light of common sense and our own sense of what was just and right.'

Beames and his district officer usually worked a thirteen-hour day. They were up and about at five in the morning. They went out on horseback inspecting roads, bridges, police stations and drains, and decided disputes about land ownership on the spot. When they got back, they had to write reports, and after that they were in court from ten in the morning until six at night.

Home and leisure

Aberigh Mackay, a visitor from Britain, described a typical district officer's house as 'a long rambling bungalow furnished with folding chairs and tables'. The verandah was 'full of fat men in clean linen waiting for interviews'. They were 'bankers, shop-keepers and land-holders', who

▼ A courtroom in the Punjab. The district officer sits at his desk. His clerks squat on the floor beside him. People with cases to be heard have to remain on the other side of the rail. (From a picture drawn in 1888)

had come to pay their respects and ask a favour. The visitors' camels lay in a circle near the bungalow, 'making bubbling noises'. One man had come on an elephant, which was standing under a tree picking up leaves with its trunk and throwing them onto its back. The visitors had brought gifts of bowls of nuts or sweets. In the eighteenth century, officials of the East India Company used to accept large bribes, and many made a fortune. Civil servants were not allowed to accept valuable gifts. If they did, they could be dismissed.

When they had time, many district officers enjoyed the sport of pig-sticking. The officer went out on horseback armed with a spear, and hunted about until he found a wild boar. He chased it, often for miles, until it turned to fight. Then he 'stuck' it with his spear. It was an exciting and exhausting sport. Wild boars could run as fast as a horse could gallop, and had sharp tusks which could injure the legs of both the horse and its rider if they got too close. Pig-sticking was a welcome change from reading and writing reports, settling disputes and inspecting drains.

The importance of the district officer
Aberigh Mackay wrote that to the people of India the district officer *was* the Government. 'He watches over their welfare, he establishes schools, dispensaries, jails and courts.' He also fixed rents and prices, and appointed every public employee in his district—from the road-sweeper to the policeman and court officials. Most district officers enjoyed their work, and when they retired many of them stayed in India.

The Indian Army

The British kept a large army in India. Part of its job was to defend India's frontiers. The most dangerous border was in the north-west, which was sometimes invaded by Afghan tribes who had to be driven out.

Troops were needed to impress the independent Indian princes, and prevent them from breaking their treaties with the British. The Army could also be used to crush riots and rebellions.

Before the Indian Mutiny (see page 110), only one in nine soldiers was British. The rest were Indian. After the Mutiny the ratio was increased to one in three. Most of the British troops came from regiments based in Britain. They served five years in India, and then returned home.

Army accommodation

Indian barracks
The death-rate among British troops in India was very high. Every year seven out of every 100 died. A government commission which began work in 1861 discovered the reasons for this high death-rate: barracks were very unhealthy places. The walls were made of wooden laths covered with plaster, and the floors were a mixture of earth and cow dung. They were overcrowded. Most barracks had no lavatories. Many had no wash rooms. At one barracks, the men washed in earthenware pie-dishes on a wooden bench in the open air.

The water supply was usually infected. When a barracks was built, Indians flocked to the site and set up businesses as shop-keepers, shoe-makers, tailors and laundrymen. They lived crowded together around the barracks. They had no drains. They threw all their sewage and rubbish into the streets and it often got into the barracks' water supply. At Bangalore the drinking water tank was filled from water that ran through the streets of a crowded town with 125,000 inhabitants. In almost every barracks the drinking water tank was used by the soldiers as a bath.

▲ British newspapers printed detailed accounts of the Indian Army's campaigns. This drawing from *The Illustrated London News* shows troops on a rough road in Afghanistan

Military hospitals

Military hospitals were worse than barracks. The walls were often canvas, with a few poles holding up a flimsy roof. There were no nurses. An untrained Indian looked after each ward. Every hospital was allowed one tub and one basin for every 100 men, and the Indians washed their patients by pouring water over them from a tin can.

Even men who were well enough to get up had to stay in bed all day, because there was nowhere in the hospital where they could sit or stroll. Hospitals were very unhealthy. The lavatories stank and overflowed. Injured men found that their wounds went septic. Most patients got worse and died. Soldiers who were ill dreaded being sent to hospital. They knew they were more likely to recover if they stayed in the barracks.

Other quarters

Married quarters, where soldiers with wives and children lived, were as bad as barracks. Only one in four of the children born to soldiers' wives in India lived to the age of five.

The soldiers' life

The daily life of the troops was very unhealthy. In hot weather they were usually confined to barracks from eight in the morning to five at night. They had nothing to do and nowhere to go, so they lay on their beds all day.

Their main recreation was drinking. Spirits were on sale in barrack canteens and in local bazaars. Officers took it for granted that their men would get drunk, and in some military hospitals in India, nearly half the patients were suffering from illnesses caused by drink.

So the 1861 Commission reported that the high death-rate among British soldiers in India was due to the insanitary state of the barracks in which they lived, and the fact that they drank too much and took too little exercise.

Officers were much better off. They lived some distance from the barracks in comfortable quarters. They had a good diet, servants to wait on them, and plenty to do in their spare time. Outdoors they played polo. Indoors they had rooms for cards and billiards.

Florence Nightingale's advice

The 1861 Commission took advice from Florence Nightingale, who had become famous for nursing sick and injured troops during the Crimean War in 1854. Florence Nightingale admired the courage of the men she had nursed, and thought that soldiers were very unfairly treated. In particular she was shocked by the unhealthy state of their barracks, and worked hard to improve their design.

She told the Commission that new barracks should be built for the Army in India, and she drew up several designs to suit different parts of the country. But she also warned that the troops would never be really fit as long as the Indian towns surrounding the barracks were unhealthy. She wrote to the India Office in London, to the viceroy and to the governors of the Indian provinces, trying to persuade them to supply the towns with pure water, proper drains and good hospitals. She wrote, 'Bombay, it is true, has a better water supply; but it has no drainage. Calcutta is being drained, but it has no water supply. Madras has neither.'

Sir Bartle Frere, Governor of Bombay, took Florence Nightingale's advice and insisted that

▲ A new barracks, built in India after the 1861 Report

Bombay's drains were improved. By the time he left India in 1867, the death-rate in Bombay was the same as in London, which was the healthiest city in Europe.

But most of Florence Nightingale's plans for improving conditions came to nothing. In London, officials at the War Office quarrelled with officials at the India Office over who was responsible for designing the new barracks. In the end the Royal Engineers built barracks designed by men who had never been to India, and who ignored what the Commission had said.

The new barracks were all the same. They had two storeys with handsome stone fronts and slate roofs. A doctor working for the Indian Government visited one and described it as 'a great palace without any kind of shelter from the sun'. Lord Napier, the Commander-in-Chief of the Army, said that in most parts of India the upper floors of the barracks were never cool. The heat of the sun on the slate roofs 'made them intolerable. They scorched the tops of the men's heads'. There was no water laid on, and no drains, and once again civilians were allowed to come and live all round the barracks.

So the new buildings were as unhealthy as the old. But they were much more expensive. A doctor at the War Office was very angry at the waste of money. He wrote, 'Fine costly architecture is no part of sanitary construction. . . . You want plain walls, watertight roofs and the deepest verandahs.'

It was even more difficult to improve conditions in towns in India. Some officials in the India Office in London agreed that drains ought to be laid and pure water supplied, but they usually said it would cost too much. Occasionally, however, they wrote to the viceroy and his council, ordering them to begin work. If the viceroy took no notice, the officials were helpless. Reports were sent to and fro, but nothing was done.

Study 5

Use your imagination

1 Private O'Hara's regiment is stationed at Bangalore. Describe a day in O'Hara's life.
Mention:
>   sitting around in the barracks,
>   a visit to his friend in hospital,
>   the native bazaar he wanders around.

(Think of a time when you felt hot, tired, uncomfortable and bored.)

2 Write the letter that Florence Nightingale might have written to the India Office in June 1871, urging the officials to make soldiers' barracks healthier and more comfortable.
Mention:
>   the reasons for the high death-rate among
>   British soldiers in India,
>   the reasons why the new barracks are no
>   better than the old,
>   the need for clean water and hospitals in
>   Indian towns.

(Think of a time when you asked for something urgent to be done quickly but no one seemed to take any notice of what you were saying.)

3 Major John Nicholson is on leave in England after serving on the North-West Frontier. His young cousin is thinking of joining the Army and asks Nicholson if he thinks that being an officer in the Indian Army is a worthwhile career. Write the answer that Nicholson might have given his cousin.
Mention:
>   the kind of job he is given to do,
>   his efforts to improve conditions for the men
>   he commands,
>   how he spends his leisure time,
>   the kind of person that he thinks would make
>   a good officer.

(Think of a time when you have tried to give an honest answer to someone who asked your advice.)

Study 6

The Suez Canal and India

The Suez Canal was opened in 1869. It was designed by a French engineer called Ferdinand de Lesseps, and the French provided much of the money that was needed to build it. In 1875 the British Prime Minister, Disraeli, took the opportunity to buy a large number of shares in the Suez Canal Company. This gave the British control of the canal and any ships passing through it.

Before the canal was opened the voyage from London to Bombay (via the Cape of Good Hope) took four to six months, but after 1869 the P&O passenger liners that used the Suez route could reach India in ninety days. The passengers could hardly bear the heat when the ships sailed through the Red Sea and across the Indian Ocean. A fierce sun beat down from a cloudless sky, shimmering on the waves with a dazzling light. Merchant ships trading with China, Australia and New Zealand also began to use the canal, and it became one of the world's most important shipping routes.

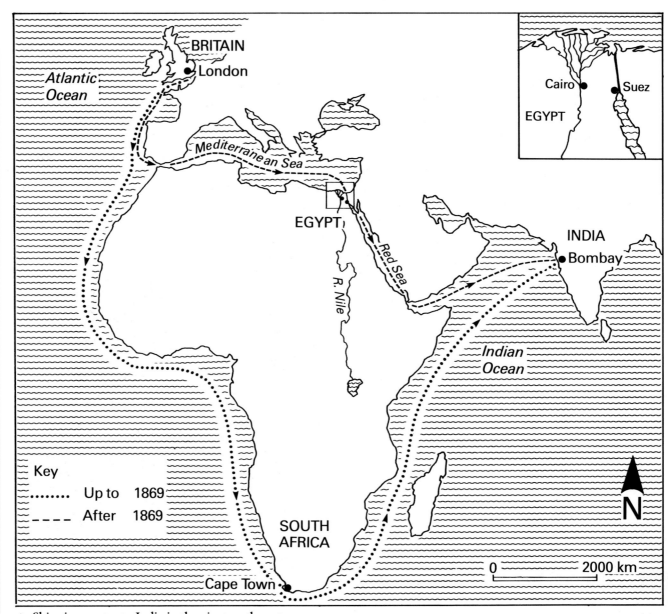

Key
- ········· Up to 1869
- - - - - - After 1869

▲ Shipping routes to India in the nineteenth century

In 1882 the British invaded Egypt because they were afraid an unfriendly Egyptian Government might take over the canal. Egypt did not become completely independent again until 1954, when all British troops were withdrawn from the country.

1 Draw the map showing shipping routes from Britain to India opposite.
  (a) Look at your map. Which country does the Suez Canal run through?
  (b) Which country did Ferdinand de Lesseps, the designer of the canal, come from?
  (c) How did Britain gain control of the canal in 1875?

2 (a) Name the two seas shown on the map that are linked by the canal.
  (b) How long did a ship take to travel from London to Bombay by way of
        the Cape of Good Hope,
        the Suez Canal?
  (c) Travellers from Bombay to London were often relieved when their ship left the Red Sea and entered the Suez Canal. Explain why.

3 (a) Why did the British invade Egypt in 1882?
  (b) How long did the British occupy Egypt?
  (c) How might an enemy who gained control of the canal have slowed down communications between Britain and India?

Civilian life

Calcutta society

All the most important government officials, their advisers and the army officers lived in Calcutta with their wives and families. While the men were out at work the women had little or nothing to do because they had Indian servants to look after them. There was an *ayah*, or nursemaid, to look after the children, a cook, a butler, a housekeeper, a gate-keeper, a groom and a number of other servants to clean and polish. Most of the British women did not speak any Indian language, so they spent their time reading, resting and exchanging visits with the wives of other officials.

They could not take much exercise because the climate was too hot. It was also very unhealthy, and as a rule at the age of four their children were sent back to Britain to a boarding school, away from dangerous tropical diseases. Many British children born in India never got to know their parents. Up to the age of four their Indian ayah looked after them. Then they went to Britain until their education was complete. Some of them found their life very boring.

▲ Two English children on their ponies, with the *syce* (Indian groom)

Life on a hill station

The migration to Simla

During the summer months it was so hot and humid in Calcutta that the British found it difficult to do any work. So in 1863 the viceroy, Sir John Lawrence, decided that in the hottest months of the year the Government would move into the hills at Simla, nearly 2,000 km away. He thought that in the clear, sharp mountain air officials would do six or seven times as much work as in the heat of Calcutta. So every year, in summer, the viceroy and all the most important officials and ambassadors, with their wives and families, went to Simla accompanied by wagon-loads of files and documents. Then every autumn they all returned to Calcutta.

Simla lay at a height of 2,150 m in the foothills of the Himalayas. In winter the climate was cold, with a good deal of snow, but in summer it was warm and pleasant. The slopes were covered with pines, oaks and rhododendrons, and cherries, apricots, raspberries and strawberries all grew well. Though there were leopards and bears in the woods, Simla was in some ways like parts of Britain, and one writer described the pleasure of seeing moss and ivy on tree-trunks and 'English wild flower and fern underfoot'.

Home life in Simla

There were always more women than men in Simla because some officials had to stay on duty in Calcutta during the summer, and they sent their wives and children for a few weeks' holiday at a bungalow in the hills. In 1890 a visitor described one of these bungalows:

'It is a cottage with a verandah, built on a steep slope and buried deep in shrubbery and trees. Within all is plain, but exquisitely neat. A wood fire is burning gaily, and the kindly tea-tray is at hand. It is five o'clock. Clean servants move silently about with hot water, cake etc. A little boy is sitting after the fashion of Anglo-Indian children in a little chair. His bearer crouches behind him while his mother in a tea-gown holds a piece of chocolate in her hand.'

Some children lived at Simla for several years because their parents did not think they were strong enough to make the long voyage back to Britain to go to school. These children were waited on hand and foot. A visitor wrote in 1886 that she found eleven servants attending one child. He never had to do anything for himself.

▲ Simla

Servants dressed him, fed him and carried him about. This treatment often made the children very selfish.

Entertainments in Simla

There was plenty to do in Simla. Families went for rides and picnics. Men went shooting in the woods. Women sketched or painted the mountain scenery. In a nearby valley there was a racecourse where horse races were held regularly in the summer. People spent much time visiting friends and giving supper parties. The food was almost always the same—preserved soup and fish from tins and jars sent out from England. No British lady would ever serve Indian food to her guests. A journalist who visited India in 1880 wrote that the English who lived there surrounded themselves as far as they could 'with an English atmosphere' and 'defended themselves' against the 'magic of the land' by organising games like croquet and archery, by joining clubs, and by attending church.

Some ladies, accompanied by their servants, went on shopping expeditions to the town's bazaars, looking for bargains among the cloths, wood-carvings and metalwork brought to Simla by Indian and Tibetan pedlars. The streets of the town were very narrow. There was no room for carriages, so the British were pulled through the streets in rickshaws.

At night some ladies and gentlemen attended amateur performances at the Gaiety Theatre, where the viceroy had a special box. Some men preferred to go to a club where they could drink, smoke and play billiards. Many stayed at home to read, chat or play cards.

On Sundays the British went to church. Christchurch, which was completed in 1857, was designed to look like an ordinary English parish church. It stood on a wide, flat terrace where the congregation used to stroll before and after the service. The terrace was also used for military parades. It was the only piece of flat ground in Simla that was big enough.

The growth of Simla

The settlement at Simla grew very quickly. In the summer of 1840 about 3,000 Indians lived in the district, and there were only 100 British visitors. The only way up to Simla was a rough path, and most supplies and visitors were carried up by porters known as *coolies*. Supplies were packed in boxes. Visitors rode up in chairs slung on poles. By 1860 a cart road had been built, and it became easier and cheaper to bring supplies. So the number of shops and houses began to grow. But most houses were very small, and even Peterhoff, the house where the viceroy stayed, had only five bedrooms.

Peterhoff was not nearly grand enough, and in 1888 a huge new lodge was built for the viceroy on a nearby hilltop. The gardens of the lodge were so large that fifty-four men were needed to keep them in order. Ten of them worked full-time to stop monkeys damaging the plants.

In 1903, when a railway was opened to Simla, 38,000 people spent the summer there. One viceroy, Lord Curzon, thought it was now too bustling and too public. His wife found the town, with its corrugated iron roofs, 'monstrous'. So they and their staff camped in tents in the mountains 21 km away.

Study 7

A guidebook to Simla

When the railway made travel faster and easier, more people began to visit distant places for pleasure. Guidebooks were printed, telling travellers how to reach the towns they were interested in and something about the way people there lived.

Use a double page to make a section of a guidebook to Simla that might have been published in about 1905. Your guide should include information on

    the climate, plants, trees and animals,
    population in the summer,
    transport to and in Simla,
    bungalows and food for guests,
    amusements.

Illustrate your guidebook.

Study 8

Back to England: Hove, 1850 – 1900

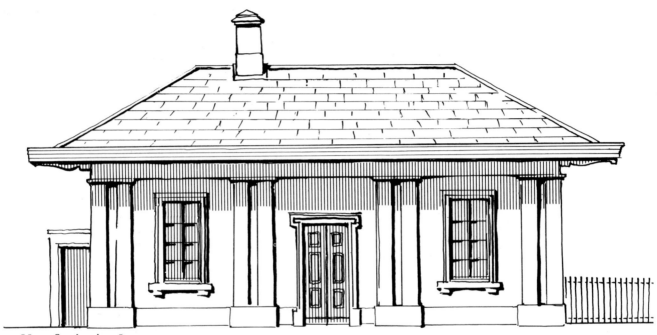

▲ Hove Station in 1841

George Holmes was an officer in the Bengal Staff Corps. When he left India and returned to England, he went to live in the new seaside resort of Hove in Sussex. In Hove he met a number of retired officers and civil servants who had served in India. Many of them had brought their Indian servants with them.

Most of George Holmes's neighbours were businessmen, doctors and lawyers who worked in London for part of the week and spent the rest of their time with their families on the coast. It was easy to travel to and fro because a railway had been built in 1841, linking London with Hove. Wealthy Londoners liked to get away from the grime and smoky atmosphere of their city, just as the British in Calcutta took the train to Simla to escape from the heat of summer. After the railway was built, more people wanted to live in Hove and from 1850 onwards the town grew rapidly.

Life in Hove was pleasant for a middle-class family. The parents and their children lived in an elegant villa or a tall terraced house, large enough to hold them and their servants. In the mornings the ladies strolled on the lawns by the sea or shopped in one of the large department stores. After a leisurely lunch, they might rest at home before going with their husbands to the theatre or to dine with friends.

On Sundays most families went to St John the Baptist Church, which was completed in 1854. The church was built by an enterprising Jewish businessman who then sold it to the Church of England. He had seen the new houses going up in the area and knew that the people who came to live in them would want a church nearby. George Holmes used to go to this church, and on its south wall there is a brass memorial plaque, put up by his family when he died in 1897.

▼ A nineteenth-century seaside villa. The iron canopy shaded the family's sitting-room. Servants prepared meals in the basement kitchen

2 Write a paragraph under the heading 'Living by the seaside, 1850–1900'.
Mention:
    how the owner of a seaside villa might have earned his living,
    ways in which the mistress of the house passed her time,
    the reason why some villa owners had Indian servants.

3 Write a paragraph under the heading 'Hove's new church, 1854–1897'.
Mention:
    why Hove needed a new church in the 1850s,
    how the church came to be built and sold to the Church of England,
    how we know that an officer who had served in India attended the church in the late nineteenth century.

1 Draw the picture of Hove railway station opposite.
Write a paragraph under the heading 'By rail to the coast, 1841–1900'.
Mention:
    why Londoners went to the coast,
    how Hove rapidly grew into a seaside resort after 1850.

▶ St John the Baptist Church, Hove. It is built in a style known as 'neo-Gothic', which copied the buildings of the Middle Ages

Trade and industry

▲ East India Dock in London, where ships trading with India were loaded and unloaded. The docks were built at the beginning of the nineteenth century

British traders in India

Many British people went to India to make money from trade. Civil servants and army officers looked down on them. They called all merchants 'box wallahs', because traders made their living buying and selling boxes of goods.

India's trade and industry were under British control, and the British made sure that Britain's interests came first. For instance, until the end of the eighteenth century, handmade Indian cotton goods had been shipped to Britain. But then Lancashire craftsmen began to use machines to make cotton cloth. They bought raw cotton from America because it was stronger and cleaner than Indian cotton. By 1832 they were exporting cotton goods to India which were sold more cheaply than anything the Indian hand-spinners and weavers could produce. So the Indian cotton industry almost died out.

In 1861 a civil war broke out in America, and Lancashire manufacturers could no longer obtain American cotton. So they demanded raw cotton from India. The Indians planted huge areas with cotton, and between 1863 and 1865 they exported cotton worth £36.5 million to England. Often the cotton replaced food crops. This resulted in food shortages in India. As soon as the American Civil War ended the mill owners began to buy American cotton again, leaving the Indians with a huge amount of raw cotton on their hands.

Tea-planting

Tea-planting and jute-making both expanded in India in the nineteenth century. Up to 1853 there was a duty of at least 4 shillings (48 old pence) per kilo on all tea imported into Britain. Then the duty was gradually reduced until in 1890 it was about 8 old pence. As the duty went down the demand went up, and the amount of tea imported into Britain increased.

Many hilly areas in India are suitable for growing tea, and adventurous young men went from Britain to set up as tea-planters. They bought land, and persuaded some of the local inhabitants to sign contracts to work on the plantations planting, picking and packing tea.

Planters promised high wages and good conditions, but they often treated their workers badly. The Indians lived in shacks and were forced to work long hours. They were badly paid, and were flogged if they did not work hard enough. Some ran away, but the planters employed special agents to round them up and bring them back. Tea-planters grew rich and powerful. They formed the Planters' Association to protect the tea trade.

The jute industry

Jute is a fibre made from the bark of a plant which grows well in parts of India and Russia. It can be made into coarse cloth suitable for making sacks

At first raw jute was exported from India to Dundee for processing, but in 1854 a manufacturer from Dundee set up a mill in Bengal near Serampore, north of Calcutta. It was an ideal site for a factory. It was close to the port of Calcutta, and there was coal nearby to provide fuel for the steam engines which drove the machinery. Other mills were established, all using machinery imported from Scotland. Most of the managers also came from Scotland. By 1908 there were thirty-eight jute companies in the Calcutta area, providing work for nearly 200,000 Indians.

The jute trade was very profitable, and the mill owners exported their sacks all over the world. But working conditions were unhealthy and dangerous. The mills were dark and stuffy. The machines were too close together. The Indians worked for low wages in ten- or twelve-hour shifts. The air was full of dust, and many workers fell ill.

Government control of industry

The Government in India passed laws which reduced hours of work and improved conditions in the mills and on the plantations. This took many years, because planters and mill owners were powerful men and had friends in the Government. They opposed all such laws. It was also very difficult to enforce the new laws because most workers could not read, and had no way of finding out what their rights were.

Canals and railways

The Indian Government itself planned and carried out two great industrial schemes—the building of canals and railways. The purpose of the canals was to irrigate the land, increase crops and prevent famine. A canal was built to take water from the River Ganges and distribute it over a wide area. Another canal irrigates over a million hectares in the Punjab, turning desert into fertile land. By 1909 the British had built nearly 20,000 km of canals in India, irrigating ten million hectares—half the size of Britain.

The Government built railways for a number of reasons. Railways help to prevent famine. Before there were railways in India, grain was carried in bullock carts. In a famine, bullocks, as well as

▲ Tea-pickers' pay depended on how much tea they picked. Here their baskets of tea are being weighed

▼ The locomotives used on Indian railways were made in India. The engine works at Jamalpur employed 10,000 men

people, starved and died. Then there was no way to transport the grain. Railways altered the situation. They could quickly bring food from where it was plentiful.

Railways were useful for moving troops. It took six months to march a regiment from Calcutta to Peshawar. A train could move the regiment in six days. Railways also encouraged trade and industry by shifting goods quickly and cheaply, making the whole country more prosperous. They also made it possible for ordinary people to travel in search of work, or for recreation. They enabled Indian people to get to know their country, and helped to unify it.

At first the Indian Government took it for granted that private companies would build the railways. But it was difficult for the companies to make a profit, and very few railways were built. In 1869 the authorities decided that the only way to build a countrywide system of railways was to do it themselves. So the Government took over.

Railway-builders in India had to overcome many problems. The bridge over the Ganges at Patna is about 3 km long, to give the river room when it is swollen by the monsoon rains. The railway east of Bombay has to climb hills nearly 1,000 m high. Forty thousand men worked to complete the line. Nearly half of them died before it was finished. But by 1909 there were more than 50,000 km of railway in India, and almost every lowland village was less than 80 km from a station.

India after the British

From about 1900 the Indian National Congress —representing the Hindus—and the Muslim League—which represented the Muslims— campaigned for the British to leave India. In 1947 the British at last left. After they had gone, the country was divided into two separate states— India, where most people were (and still are) Hindus, and Pakistan, where most people were Muslims. But in 1971 Bengalis living in East Pakistan set up a new independent state called Bangladesh. So now the former British colony of India is split into three separate nations, each with its own system of government.

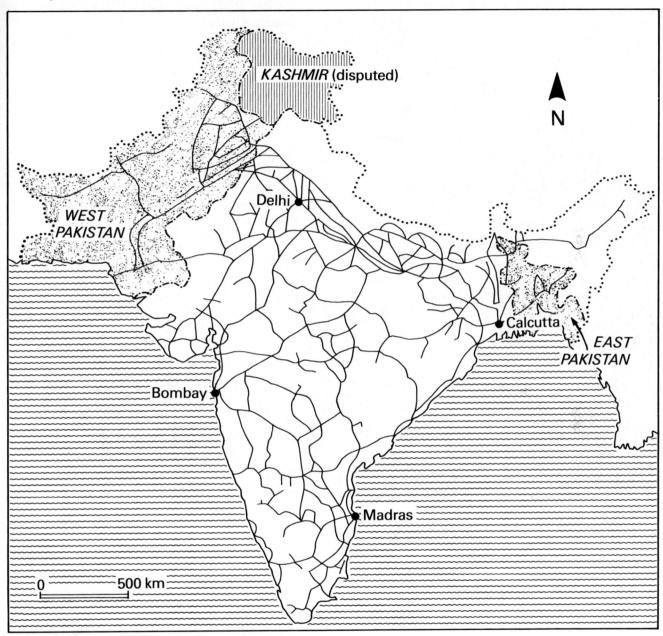

▲ India and West and East Pakistan in 1947, showing the railway network

Study 9

British trade with India

1 *In pairs:* find one or more pieces of information to support or explain each of the following statements about trade and industry in India, and Britain in the nineteenth century.

   (a) Indians could buy some goods that were imported from Britain more cheaply than they could buy similar goods made in India.

   (b) British people with money to invest set up industries in India that provided work for thousands of Indians.

   (c) After 1854, many Scots who worked in the jute mills of Dundee lost their jobs because their factories closed down.

   (d) In the 1860s the demand for raw cotton in Britain led to food shortages in India.

2 Use the information that you have gathered to decide whether or not you agree with this statement:

   'In the nineteenth century, India's trade and industry were under British control and the British made sure that Britain's interests came first.'

   Be ready to give your reasons for reaching your decision.

3 Ask one person who agrees with the statement in question 2, and one who disagrees with it, to give their reasons for doing so. What do the rest of you think?

Study 10

'Rawalpindi'—a British bungalow, 1920

▲ Unlike Indian bungalows, most British bungalows did not have a verandah

In India many people live in *bungalas* or bungalows—houses where all the rooms are built in one long row, on a platform raised a few feet above ground level. The rooms open out onto a shady verandah.

In Britain in the 1920s and 1930s, builders used the name 'bungalow' to describe the one-storied houses that they were putting up along the roads that ran from the towns into the countryside. Each bungalow had a front garden, and a large garden at the back that often looked onto fields. The houses were wired for electricity so the owners could use labour-saving appliances such as vacuum cleaners and electric ovens. It was easy to get into town by the buses that ran past the door or by the family motorcar.

British people who had retired from working in India and returned to Britain often chose to live in a bungalow. Some called their new homes 'Rawalpindi' or 'Simla' to remind them of their old lives, and furnished their rooms with screens, teak tables and carved ivory ornaments.

Make a display

A firm of British builders is holding a competition to see who can design the best window-display advertising the bungalows it is building.

The aim of the display is to persuade possible customers that bungalows are easy to run, and that they give their owners the feeling that they are living in India.

The display must include:
> a slogan,
> the groundplan of an Indian bungalow,
> an artist's impression of a row of British bungalows,
> a list of the advantages of living in a bungalow.

In groups of three or four: prepare an entry for the competition. Display your work and decide who has won the competition.

Further work

Writing

1 Copy the statements below and add an example to illustrate each of them:
> British people in India had plenty of servants.
> Few Indians held important jobs in the civil service.
> The British kept control over the Indians in the Indian Army.

2 Under the heading 'The British and India', write two paragraphs explaining why each of these years was important in the history of India and Britain:

1857   1947

3 Write an essay under the heading 'British rule in India':

(a) Make brief notes to show how the British
> helped India and its people (give two or more examples),
> kept control over the Indian people (give two or more examples),
> kept themselves apart from the Indians.

(b) Turn your notes into three paragraphs.

(c) Many Indians were pleased when their country became independent in 1947.
Write a conclusion to your essay saying *why* the Indians wanted their independence.

Drawing

1 (a) Draw the map of India in 1947 on page 129, leaving out the railways.

(b) Write a sentence about each of these towns, explaining why it was important to the British in India:
> Calcutta   Simla   Bombay

2 (a) Draw a picture for a postcard that might have been sent home by a British visitor to India in about 1890.

(b) Write a message of about thirty words and the address that might have been written on the card.

3 (a) Draw three 'photographs' that might have been found in the photograph album of a British man or woman who worked in India between 1870 and 1900.

(b) Write a caption to go with each picture.

Drama
Give the talk that might have been given by a British man or woman who was home on leave from India in about 1905.

In groups of three:
1 Choose a different subject each, for example, 'My first tiger hunt'.
2 Prepare brief notes for a talk to last between one and two minutes.
3 Give your talk to the people in your group.
4 Choose two groups to give their talks to the class.

6 Inquiry
The Irish Potato Famine
'Want in the midst of plenty'

Skibbereen

Skibbereen is a small town in the south-west of Ireland. In December 1846 it was like a ghost town. No sounds came from the rough, one-roomed cabins where the poor people lived: no one was about in the streets.

On about 17 December an official called Richard Inglis arrived in Skibbereen to investigate reports that people there were dying of hunger. Before he had gone very far he had to stop and help to bury three dead bodies that were lying in the street. Officials in the town told him that during the last six weeks about a hundred bodies, half-eaten by rats, had been picked up in the narrow lanes that ran between the rows of cabins, and that another 197 people had died in the local workhouse.

Richard Inglis knew that more lives would be lost unless he acted quickly. He had collected £85 to buy food for people who could not afford to buy it for themselves. With this money he and his helpers set up two soup kitchens and before long, hundreds of starving men, women and children came flocking to them, begging for something to eat. They were shivering from exhaustion and fever and had wrapped ragged shawls and blankets around their frail bodies in an attempt to keep out the cold. Thanks to Richard Inglis, some of them survived but many were too weak and ill to live for more than a few days.

1 Where is Skibbereen?
2 Why did Richard Inglis go there in December 1846?
3 Did Richard Inglis obtain reliable evidence to confirm the reports he had received? Give reasons for your answer.

Protestant settlers in Ireland

In 1846 the whole of Ireland formed part of Great Britain—the richest country in the world. Yet even though Britain was rich in that year thousands of poor Irish peasants starved to death. It seemed to them that the British did not care what happened to them.

In the seventeenth century, Protestant settlers from the mainland had taken over most of the land. Since then, Ireland had been ruled as if it was almost a British colony. By 1700 more than three-quarters of the land was owned by Protestants. The few Catholics who still owned land had estates in the west of Ireland where the land was difficult to farm. Most people living in northern Ireland were Protestants, but the vast majority of people in the south were Catholics.

Irish Catholics

Irish Catholics were treated very badly in the eighteenth century. They could not vote or become MPs, and they were not allowed to hold any government post. Gradually they were given more rights: for example, in 1793 Catholic landowners got the vote, and after 1829 they could become MPs.

1 Copy the statements that are correct.
   In 1846
      all of Ireland was united with mainland Britain,

      most of the land in Ireland was owned by Protestants whose ancestors came from mainland Britain,

      the majority of people living in northern Ireland were Catholics.

2 Why may the Protestant settlers in the seventeenth century have allowed the Catholics to keep the land in the west?
3 Would you expect most of the people of Skibbereen in 1846 to have been Catholics or Protestants? Give reasons for your answer.

After the Famine, many Irish people, both Catholics and Protestants, believed that the British Government was only interested in looking after the people who lived in mainland Britain, and did not care what happened to the people of Ireland. They thought the Irish people would be better off if they were given control over their own affairs.

Was it the British Government's fault that so many Irish peasants died? See what you think at the end of this Inquiry.

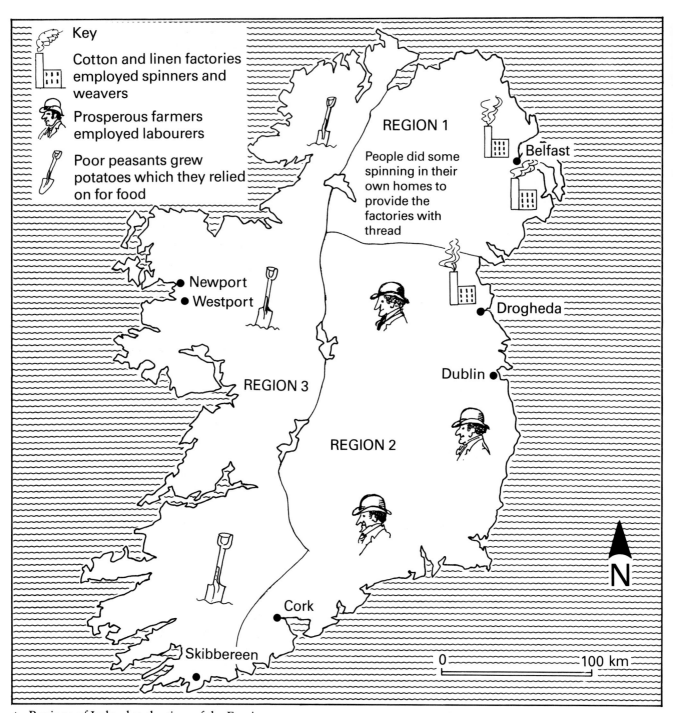

Key

Cotton and linen factories employed spinners and weavers

Prosperous farmers employed labourers

Poor peasants grew potatoes which they relied on for food

REGION 1

People did some spinning in their own homes to provide the factories with thread

Belfast

Newport
Westport

Drogheda

Dublin

REGION 3

REGION 2

Cork

N

Skibbereen

0   100 km

▲ Regions of Ireland at the time of the Famine

The regions of Ireland

1 Look at the map of Ireland opposite.
  (a) List the main ways in which people in each of the three regions shown on the map made a living.
  (b) How did the people in the Skibbereen area make a living?
2 Look at the map and Source 1.
  (a) Why had the people of Westport and Newport once been able to afford a 'comfortable' standard of living?
  (b) By 1837, one of the jobs they had once done had been taken over by factory workers in Region 1. Which job was it?

Source 1

> 'In the district about Westport and Newport the people were formerly in comfortable circumstances, uniting the occupations of farmer, weaver and fisherman.'
>
> *(Report, 1837)*

3 Which of the three regions do you think was
    the richest,
    the poorest?
  Give reasons for your answer.

The peasants of the west

Much of the land in the west of Ireland is made up of mountains and peat bogs. It is difficult to grow corn there, so the peasants grew potatoes instead. They dug up the crop every autumn and stored most of the potatoes to provide them with food for the coming year. Even when the harvest was good their stocks were usually low by the next summer.

1 Read Source 2.
  (a) What did the peasants eat at mealtimes?
  (b) What are we told that shows the peasants were generous and trusting?
2 Read Source 3.
  (a) How many people were unemployed for thirty weeks of every year?
  (b) Why did they work for only twenty-two weeks every year?
3 Read Source 4.
  Explain in your own words why peasants in the west of Ireland needed children.

Source 2

> 'The neighbour or the stranger finds every man's door open and to walk in without ceremony at meal time and to partake of his bowl of potatoes is always sure to give pleasure.'
> Sir John Carr
>
> (Written in about 1800)

Source 3

> '... for thirty weeks of the year, that is, ... except when the potatoes were being cultivated, 2,385,000 persons were without employment because there was absolutely no work to offer them.'
> Cecil Woodham Smith
> (From *The Great Hunger*, published in 1962)

Source 4

> '... in pre-famine Ireland children were a necessity ... a man and woman's insurance against destitution in their old age.'
> Cecil Woodham Smith
> (From *The Great Hunger*, published in 1962)

What do you think?

Many people in Britain thought the Irish were careless, lazy and had too many children, so it was their own fault if they were poor.
1 Did the British have any reason to believe this?
2 Were the peasants to blame if they were poor? Give reasons for your answers.

The British Government and the Famine

In the autumn of 1845 the potato harvest in the south and west of Ireland was destroyed by blight. This disease had spread among the plants while they were growing, and turned the potatoes into a black, stinking pulp. When people realised how far the disease had spread they knew that there would be a terrible famine. There were no potatoes to import to replace the crops that had been destroyed, but the Government thought it would be possible to import corn. Table 1 shows you what the Government planned to do about the Famine and how it put its plan into action.

1 (a) Why did the peasants in the west eat so many potatoes?

(b) Why was it clear, in the autumn of 1845, that there would be a terrible famine?

2 (a) Look at Table 1. What action did the Government take

(i) to help traders to import cheap foreign corn,

(ii) to encourage landlords to find food grown in Ireland for their tenants?

(b) What did the Government do to help peasants in the worst famine areas to buy food?

3 (a) Which of these statements do you think sums up the Government's aims?

To take control of all food supplies for Ireland, and make sure that everyone had a fair share of what food there was.

To attract supplies of food to the markets in Ireland by encouraging private enterprise and only taking direct government action in the worst famine areas.

(b) The Government thought that there was plenty of cheap corn in Europe that could be imported to Ireland, but it was wrong.

(i) From which country did the Government have to import corn?

(ii) The price of food that is scarce rises if a lot of people want to buy it. Why would you expect food prices to rise in Ireland during 1846?

Table 1

Government Plans	Government Actions
(a) To rely on private traders to import most of the corn needed in Ireland	Parliament was persuaded to change the law so that traders could import cheap foreign corn
(b) To spend a limited amount of government money on buying corn for the worst famine areas	Government agents bought £100,000 worth of American corn. It was sent to government depots in the worst famine areas
(c) To move corn from areas in Ireland that had plenty, to areas where there was a shortage	Irish landlords were told to form Relief Committees and find food for their tenants
(d) To make it possible for peasants to buy food cheaply	Government schemes provided work for the peasants and paid them wages

The Famine and the London press

In the autumn of 1846 the potato crop failed again. Articles and letters appeared in the London papers, commenting on the Irish and conditions in Ireland.

1 Read Source 5. Is the writer saying that

(a) the poor people in Ireland are no worse off than people in Scotland and England—they just make more fuss,

(b) the poor people of Ireland are in despair and people in the rest of Britain should help them?

Source 5

'... the Irishman is destitute, so is the Scotchman, and so is the Englishman ... there is nothing so peculiar, so exceptional, in the condition which they [the Irish] look on as the pit of utter despair.'

(*The Times*, 8 September 1846)

2 Look at Table 2.
  Why might a man who was working on a government scheme still have been unable to buy enough food for his family?

3 Two clergymen from Skibbereen saw officials in London on 6 December. They said there was no Relief Committee in Skibbereen, so they were trying to keep people alive by giving them soup. They begged the officials to send food to Skibbereen. No food was sent.

  Read Source 6.
  What might Nicholas Cummins have hoped to achieve by writing to *The Times*?

4 Look at the picture from *The Illustrated London News*, below.
  (a) Did the artist think that the Government

      should send food to Skibbereen,
      should not send food to Skibbereen?

    Give reasons for your answer.
  (b) What might a thoughtful reader of *The Illustrated London News* have learnt about life in Skibbereen in the January of 1847 from looking at the illustration?

Table 2

Wages and Prices, winter 1846	
Daily wage of a man employed on a government work scheme	8d
Daily cost of one meal for six people	10d

Source 6

'I entered some of the hovels ... In the first, six famished and ghastly skeletons, to all appearances dead, were huddled in a corner on some filthy straw ... I approached with horror, and found by a low moaning they were alive—they were in fever, four children, a woman and what had once been a man.'
(From a letter written by Nicholas Cummins, describing conditions in Skibbereen on 15 December and published in *The Times* on 24 December 1846)

▲ A funeral at Skibbereen during the Famine, from *The Illustrated London News*, 30 January 1847. There were no coffins left in Skibbereen by this time

Charles Trevelyan and the Famine

Charles Trevelyan was the British official in charge of Famine Relief for Ireland. He worked long and hard in his office in London to try to help the Irish. Like most people in the Government at that time, he believed that trade and industry work best when they are left to private individuals and the Government does not interfere.

1 (a) Charles Trevelyan never saw a starving Irishman or Irishwoman. Explain why not.
  (b) Did he believe in
        government control of industry and trade,
        private enterprise?

2 (a) Some Relief Committees asked if they could sell corn to the peasants in the worst famine areas at a very low price. The amount they wanted to charge for the corn was less than it cost to import it. Trevelyan refused. He believed that if he allowed the Relief Committees to do this, private traders would not be able to sell their corn, so they would stop importing it.
    Which does Trevelyan seem to have thought was more important:
        to make sure that as much corn as possible was imported to Ireland in the long run,
        to act quickly to save lives in the worst famine areas?

  (b) Some Relief Committees asked Trevelyan to send some of the corn that was stored in Britain to Ireland. Trevelyan believed that if he did this there would be a shortage of corn in Britain. The price of bread would rise and many people would be too poor to buy it. So he refused.
    Which does Trevelyan seem to have thought was more important:
        to make sure that the Irish did not starve,
        to make sure that the English, Scots and Welsh did not suffer because there was a famine in Ireland?

3 (a) Did Trevelyan try to help the Irish? Give reasons for your answer.
  (b) Do you think he turned down the requests from the Relief Committees because
        he did not think it mattered if Irish peasants died,
        he thought that if he did as the Committees asked he would only make matters worse?

The Catholics and the Famine

In 1845, before the Famine, there were about 8 million people in Ireland. After the Famine, in 1849, the population had dropped to about 5.5 million. A million and a half people had starved to death, and another million had emigrated to Britain or the United States. The Catholic peasants suffered the most. Thousands of them who survived the Famine were homeless because they could not pay their rent, and their landlords had sent men to turn them off the land and pull down their cabins. This made the peasants hate the landlords. They also hated the British Government. It had done so little to help them that they thought it wanted to get rid of them, and had deliberately allowed the Famine to kill them off.

Ireland after the Famine

After the Famine, British Governments tried to help peasants to buy farms and improve the land, but the Irish still felt bitter and angry. They wanted to decide what ought to be done themselves. Some people worked to obtain self-government by peaceful means. Others committed murders, destroyed property and raided police stations in an attempt to drive the British out of Ireland. Irish-Americans sent money and weapons to help in the struggle.

Eventually the British Government and the Irish Catholic MPs agreed that Ireland should remain united with Britain, but that the Irish should be given more say in their own affairs. The Irish Protestants bitterly opposed this idea, because they were afraid that Ireland would be governed by Catholics who would destroy the Protestant way of life. The new system was due to come into force in 1914, but when the First World War broke out in August, the Government decided to leave things as they were until the War was over.

Ireland is divided

After the First World War many small countries that had once been part of European empires were given their independence. The Catholics in Ireland thought that their country should leave the British Empire and be completely independent: but Protestants in the north were still determined not to be ruled by Catholics.

In 1922, after a civil war in Ireland, the country was divided into two. The south formed Eire, an independent republic with its capital in Dublin. Northern Ireland formed a separate province which was still united with Britain.

Problems in Northern Ireland

Some of the men in the Irish Republican Army (IRA), which had fought for Ireland's independence, thought that their leaders were wrong to let Ireland be divided, and vowed that one day they would reunite it. The Protestants in the north felt threatened by the IRA. Although Protestants were in a majority in the north, in some parts of the province, for example, in County Armagh and in the cities of Belfast and Londonderry, there were large numbers of Catholics. The Protestants watched these northern Catholics to make sure that they did not help the IRA, and tried to exclude them from power. The Catholics felt that they were treated unfairly, and were not given the same opportunities as the Protestants.

In 1968 a civil rights movement was started in Northern Ireland to try to win equal rights for everyone who lived there. At first there were peaceful demonstrations, but then fighting broke out between the Protestant and Catholic communities, and the British Government sent troops from Britain to restore order. This angered the IRA, and a campaign of killing and bombing was started, to try to drive the troops out.

The British Government, leaders in Northern Ireland, and the Government of the Irish Republic have all tried to find a solution to the problem in Northern Ireland, but so far they have not succeeded. Most Protestants in Northern Ireland think it should stay a part of the United Kingdom, but many Catholics think of it as a colony that Britain should give up.

1 Give two reasons why the population of Ireland fell from about 8 million to about 5.5 million between 1845 and 1849.
2 What happened in Ireland as a result of
   the Civil War of 1922,
   the civil rights movement of 1968?
3 Since 1849 movements against British rule in Ireland have received a great deal of support from Irish-Americans. For what reasons may Irish-Americans have opposed British rule in Ireland?

———— 7 Topic work ————

This book gives you some idea of what life was like when Britain was the centre of a great empire, but it cannot tell you about all the interesting and important events that were happening at that time. You can find out more about the British Empire between 1750 and 1950 by writing on one of these topics:

Tea, Sugar and Cotton
'Native' peoples and Settlers
Houses in Britain and the Empire
Women in Peace and War
Travel by Land and Sea
Immigrants to Britain

Do not decide on your topic yet.

Find your information
1 *Illustrations*
   (a) *In pairs:* look at the picture on page 130. Which topic does this picture illustrate?
   (b) Look through the illustrations in this book and find a picture, map or diagram to illustrate three of the other topics listed above.
2 *Writing*
   If you want to look up information on one of the topics you could begin by looking it up in the Index of this book. For example, for *Travel by Land and Sea*, you could look up the first word, *Travel*. You may also find useful information listed in the Index under another word connected with your topic. For example, you may find out something about *Immigrants to Britain* if you looked up *Jews*.
   In pairs: write a list of words that you might look up for three of the topics suggested above.

Note your information
Choose the topic that you would like to study and make notes on it, using
   (a) information from this book,
   (b) information from books in your school library.
Remember:
   (a) Look at the Contents and Index pages of a book as well as its title.
   (b) Make brief notes that you can write up later. Information that you wish to quote in the exact words used in the book *must* be put in inverted commas.
   (c) Make a note of the title and author of any book that you use.

Plan your topic
When you have collected your information, decide on three or four chapter headings for your topic. For example, if you have chosen *Tea, Sugar and Cotton* your chapters might be called:
   The tea trade
   Sugar and Victorian sweets, cakes and puddings
   Cotton factories in Britain and India
   A British family at teatime

Write your topic book
1 Write up each chapter and draw the illustrations.
2 Write an introduction saying
   (a) why you chose the topic,
   (b) which piece of information that you found surprised or interested you the most.
3 Write
   (a) a list of contents,
   (b) a bibliography, listing the books that you have used and the names of their authors.

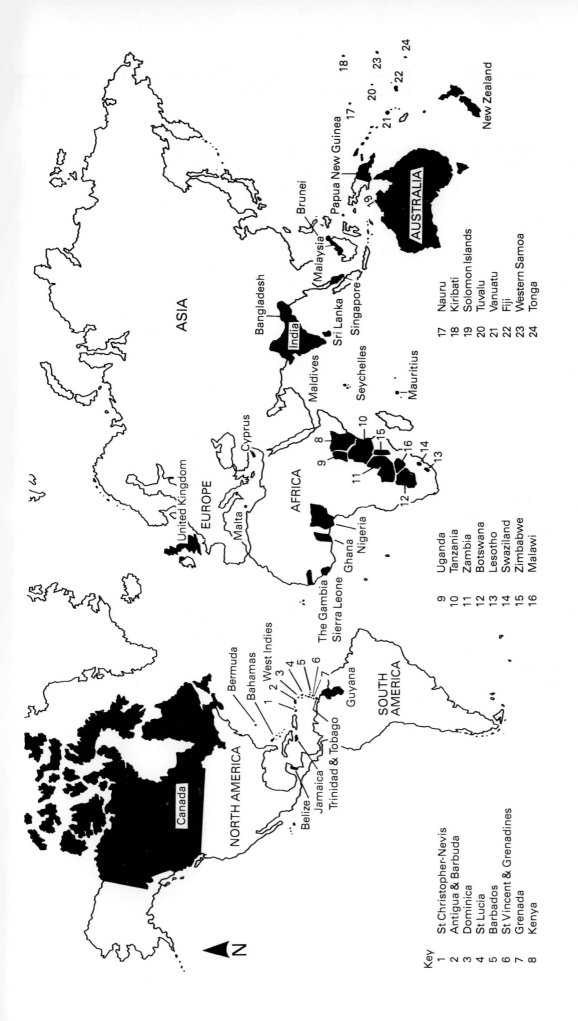

N

ASIA

EUROPE

United Kingdom

Malta

Cyprus

AFRICA

The Gambia
Sierra Leone
Ghana
Nigeria

Bangladesh
India
Maldives
Sri Lanka
Seychelles
Singapore
Mauritius

Brunei
(Malaysia)
Papua New Guinea

17
20
21
19

18
23
24
22

AUSTRALIA

New Zealand

Bermuda
Bahamas
West Indies
1
2
3
4
5
6
7
Belize
Jamaica
Trinidad & Tobago
Guyana

NORTH AMERICA

Canada

SOUTH AMERICA

Key
1 St Christopher-Nevis
2 Antigua & Barbuda
3 Dominica
4 St Lucia
5 Barbados
6 St Vincent & Grenadines
7 Grenada
8 Kenya

9   Uganda
10 Tanzania
11 Zambia
12 Botswana
13 Lesotho
14 Swaziland
15 Zimbabwe
16 Malawi

17 Nauru
18 Kiribati
19 Solomon Islands
20 Tuvalu
21 Vanuatu
22 Fiji
23 Western Samoa
24 Tonga

From Empire to Commonwealth
The countries that made up the British Empire, and were governed by the British, now govern themselves. Many of them now make up the group of countries known as the British Commonwealth. These are shown in black on the map.

Index

Page numbers in **bold** refer to illustrations.